THE CHURCH
THROUGH THE CENTURIES

AMS PRESS
NEW YORK

THE CHURCH
THROUGH *The* CENTURIES

By
CYRIL CHARLES RICHARDSON

1950
NEW YORK
CHARLES SCRIBNER'S SONS
CHARLES SCRIBNER'S SONS, Ltd., LONDON

Library of Congress Cataloging in Publication Data

Richardson, Cyril Charles, 1909-1976.
    The church through the centuries.

    Reprint of the 1938 ed. published by Scribner, New
York.
    Bibliography: p.
    Includes index.
    1. Church history. 2. Religious thought—History.
I. Title.
BR148.R56   1979   270   72-6726
ISBN 0-404-10645-5

Reprinted from the edition of 1938, New York, from an
original in the collections of the Cleveland Public Library.
[Trim size and text area of the original have been
maintained in this edition.]

MANUFACTURED
IN THE UNITED STATES OF AMERICA

PREFACE

ONE OF the most pertinent problems that confronts modern Christianity is the meaning of the Church for today. This is not a question which merely concerns theologians, nor will its answer ultimately come from the arid discussions of the learned. The meaning of the Church is implied in all our Christian work and worship. It is a vital issue for every layman, since the quality of our Christian faith and life is largely determined by what we believe the Church essentially is.

My book has been written in order to help those who desire some perspective in considering this grave problem, and who want to know something of what the Church has meant, and means today, in the divergent traditions of Christianity.

I have attempted to give some account of the historical backgrounds out of which various views of the Church have arisen, and to indicate the main lines upon which the concept of the Church has developed through the course of Christian history. I have often heard the need expressed for such a book, and I hope that my volume will prove of some value in this connection. Any book which attempts to survey so large a field is necessarily open to the criticism of over-generalization, and I trust that by the use of stories and illustrations this defect has been partially overcome.

I wish to express my gratitude to President Henry Sloane Coffin, to Professor William Adams Brown, to Doctor Edward Hardy, and to Doctor David Roberts for their kindness in reading the manuscript and offering valuable criticisms.

CYRIL C. RICHARDSON.

Union Theological Seminary,
New York,
January, 1938.

CONTENTS

THE CHURCH
THROUGH THE CENTURIES

CHAPTER I

THE MEANING OF THE CHURCH TODAY

WHAT do we mean when we speak of the "Church"? There is hardly a word in our language which has suffered more from the richness of its meaning and the variety of its interpretation. Perhaps its most usual connotation is that of the denomination. It is frequently used, however, to signify the church building,[1] or the members that compose a particular congregation. At other times it is a synonym for the ministers. We talk of the Church taking action in the social sphere, by which we generally imply that the clergy pass resolutions about the needs of our generation. To others, again, the term has the most sacred associations. It signifies the sanctuary of God, where He makes Himself peculiarly known in the corporate worship of the people of Christ. Yet another meaning can be found, one indeed, which the Greek equivalent of the word (i.e. *ekklesia*) has by derivation. It is used of those who are called by God. So it is that we speak of the Church "visible" and "invisible," distinguishing the various Christian congregations which are seen in the world from that body of God's people which He has called and chosen for salvation, and which is discerned not by the eye of sense, but by the eye of faith.

With so many possible meanings it is not surprising that this word has caused constant confusion. People often talk about the

[1] The English word "Church" is probably derived from the Greek adjective *kuriakon*, which was used absolutely for the church building (*kuriakon doma*), the house of the Lord. The English term, however, also bears the sense of the Greek word *ekklesia*, the people called by God.

I

Church without defining exactly what they mean. The purpose of this book will be to give a brief account of the various ideas that have surrounded this word through the course of history, and to illustrate them with examples of Christian life and worship. It is important to realise that the meaning of the term has changed with historical circumstances and with new modes or styles of thought, for there is a style of thought characteristic of each age— just as there is a style of dress or of architecture. This will bring us at the close face to face with the really vital problem for Christians today: What can and ought the Church to mean for our generation? It is not sufficient merely to know what the Church has meant in the past: this is but an indication of what it must mean for our Christian life and thought today. The twentieth century is not the sixteenth or the second and, while we have by our tradition much in common with the past, the most important thing that should concern us is the relation of our tradition to the present; the relation, that is, of the eternal element in Christianity to that which is unique in the life and thought of our generation. There is an immediate urgency that we should have a clear understanding of the meaning and place of the Church in our world. From a variety of sources Christianity has been attacked as outmoded and incapable of meeting the problems of our modern world. It is only as Christians become conscious of themselves as a world-wide community, sharing a divine life and a common faith, that they will be able to withstand the movements that threaten the very foundations of the Gospel of Christ.

Of such movements in our modern world we are becoming increasingly aware. The people of Russia have devoted themselves to the formation of a type of society, where the motives of private enterprise are subordinated to the general life of the State. To realise this corporate life is regarded as the final meaning of existence and what the Russian Communist really worships is man, who shares with his fellows the fruit of his labour and the luxuries of leisure. This social organisation may be enforced in a cruel and dictatorial manner, often at the expense of liberty, but the Russian government believes that the only practical way of getting things done is by the use of force.

This sense of corporate life is equally and at times even more profoundly evident in the Nazi and kindred movements of our day. The extreme anti-Christian parties in Germany confessedly worship the gods of blood and race and soil. This neo-paganism is not to be brushed aside as merely stupid and superstitious. Rather is it a recovery of something very profound and long neglected in our artificial life of cities and technical machinery. Men have been isolated by our mechanical age: they have been cut loose from their natural surroundings, the race, the blood, the soil, of which they are a part, and the recovery of these as objects of worship satisfies a need of which the modern man is deeply conscious. He feels that he has rediscovered his roots: he is part of a greater whole. The corporate nature of German life, grounded in the soil and the race, seems very real and desirable when contrasted with the loneliness and isolation of being a mechanical unit in a factory.

Now these two instances of the recovery in our modern world of the corporate sense of life, its union with nature and with our fellow men, have seriously threatened Christianity. The gods that are worshipped are not, in either case, the God of our Lord and Saviour Jesus Christ: indeed, there are elements in Christianity, such as the infinite worth of the individual as a child of God, which run counter to the Communist and Fascist trends. Yet to dismiss these movements merely as unchristian is to fail to understand the world in which we live.

There is a truth in Communism and National Socialism which we neglect at the peril of losing the true meaning of Christianity. The corporate nature of human life in association with our fellows, in sharing the gifts and luxuries of the earth, is basic to Christian faith, just as our essential union with all natural existence is a necessary element in every attempt to give meaning to life. What is both tragic and dangerous in Communism and National Socialism is not that they are fundamentally wrong, but that they are partly right. Men cannot live on lies, and no great movements in history are ever founded purely on falsehood. The demonic and unchristian element in Communism and National Socialism is that they elevate these two aspects of human life to the sphere of the divine and worship them as God. That is why they are basically opposed to Christianity, which worships one God and not many, and which regards God as above all corporate human life and sees the soil and nature and the heritage of the race not as God, but as the gifts of God to His children.

While in America these two movements are not of immediate pressing importance, a similar attempt to elevate things to the sphere of the divine can be seen in the proverbial "American dream," in which the ultimate meaning of life is regarded as the production of goods and the accumulation of wealth. These become God. It is true that selfish profit and haphazard production are today giving way to a more social sense of this ideal and there is a real concern for such basic issues as poverty and war, nevertheless the corporate prosperity of the citizens of America is not seldom interpreted as the final end of our existence.

In all these ways, then, the meaning of our life as grounded in nature and to some extent fulfilled in the corporate life with our fellowmen, is being stressed today. This has presented to Christians a definite challenge which is of a twofold nature. Firstly, if

Christians recognise that this corporate life is essential for the true fulfilment of man's nature, are they trying to live up to this profession? Are they vitally concerned about the impending war, the poverty and unemployment of their generation? And secondly, does Christianity entail anything more than this? The importance of this second challenge cannot be overemphasised. If Christianity means nothing more, its persecution by Communism and National Socialism might be justified. Through history Christian institutions have often been so closely associated with those forces that make for reaction, that it would be as well to do away with them and particularly with the superstitions which have accumulated around them during the past ages.

It may of course be objected that the difference lies not in the ultimate goal but in the way the Fascists and Communists on the one hand, and the Christians on the other, attempt to reach it. Historically, Protestant Christianity and democracy are inseparably united, and what therefore is at stake in the warfare of these three parties is the method of realising human corporate life. There might be some justification for the existence of Protestant Christian institutions as the guarantors of the democratic method and the preservers of individual liberty and freedom.

Such an approach is not uncommonly taken today and the task of Christians is seen merely in the light of their social and political activity. How infinitely different this attitude is to the classical expressions of Christian life and faith can best be appreciated by a study which begins with the Early Church. There the profound difference between Christianity and every effort concerned solely with human social organisation is to be clearly seen.

CHAPTER II

THE CHURCH IN THE LIFE AND THOUGHT OF THE EARLY CENTURIES

THE FELLOWSHIP OF SALVATION

"HE WAS," says Plato, referring to Socrates at the conclusion of the *Phædo,* "of all those of his time whom we have known, the best and wisest and most righteous man."

"Truly," exclaimed the centurion who witnessed the crucifixion of Jesus Christ, "this man was the Son of God."

The contrast implicit in these two utterances contains the secret of the early Christians. Their community was not a society for ethical culture but a fellowship of salvation. Their religion was one of reconciliation with God. They believed God had taken action in history. He had sent His Son into the world in order to remove the obstacle of sin which had previously separated men from God. The profoundest knowledge of the early Christians was not that Jesus was a good man who had given His disciples some valuable advice about God and the conduct of life, but that the searching demands Jesus had made upon men by His preaching and life could only be realised in the fellowship of a community which recognised Him as their Lord, the Saviour whom God had sent.

In attempting to understand the meaning of this we are confronted with grave difficulties. The whole tenor of modern thought has been to regard it as an axiom that man can fulfil these demands of Jesus if only he takes them seriously enough and really tries to live the good life. This position was entirely foreign to such early apostles as Saint Paul. The whole point was that man found himself in a tragic predicament. The more seriously he took the Law of Moses and applied to himself the standards of conscience and of the teachings of Jesus, the more he was conscious of his utter impotence to realise this kind of life. Christianity started not from an optimistic sense of man's capability, but from a tragic and overwhelming conviction of his failure and of his corrupt nature.

The early Christian gospel was as simple as it was profound. It claimed that God had released man from this predicament of well-wishing and incapability. He had sent into the world His Son, who became Man. By the power of His divine nature He had redeemed and restored fallen humanity, making it possible for men to have hope, and finally, under the control of the spirit of Christ, to achieve the plan that God had for His creation.

So it was that the Christians answered the ultimate question with which man is faced, the question of death. The vicious circle of natural life with its birth and decay, and of spiritual life with its insight and impotence, was broken by the Incarnation, by the coming to earth of the Son of God. Men were restored to fellowship with God because the power of sin and death was defeated.

The chief difficulty in understanding these convictions of the early Christians has been twofold. Through our technical age with its isolation of the individual, we have so long lost the sense of the corporate nature of our humanity, the fact of our mutual interdependence on one another. Yet this conviction that we are all tied up in the same bundle of life together was very real to the early Christians. It meant that if our human nature was redeemed in Christ, then it could be redeemed in all men.

A second difficulty has arisen from the fact that when we speak of nature, we think only of the physical aspect, whereas the early Christians meant by that term all of man's being, including his will. Thus they did not conceive of redemption as a purely physical process, although it was not without implications for man's body, no less than for his soul. Life in Christ was not mediated by magic or superstition. All men were not at once saved by the Incarnation. On the contrary, man unites himself with this saving power of God in Christ by an act of faith, whereby he humbly accepts his predicament as fallen and disobedient and casts himself upon the abounding mercy and love of God. The believer becomes "in Christ," under His control and submissive to Him. He discovers the power that redeems, and he knows that the ultimate meaning of life is the negation of his own selfish purposes, the losing of his life in order to gain it in Christ.

Three things, then, were clearly involved in the revelation of God in Christ. There was, first, illumination. The Christian saw in Christ God's perfect plan for man. He became aware of what God demanded of him, of what life in its highest expression of love and self-sacrifice and obedience to God could be. This was also an expression of judgment upon man's failure, his sin and sense of self-sufficiency. Then, secondly, in the Incarnation there was power. God in Christ had redeemed man and had conquered evil. This power man grasped by faith in Christ, submitting his life to the rule and dominion of God and looking in hope to the complete fulfilment of His purpose at the end of history. Lastly, there was forgiveness and the restoration of right relations with God. In Christ the love of God was revealed. God had taken action in history and had given men the confident assurance of salvation and of reconciliation with Him. In Christ God was known as Saviour as well as Judge.

This, in brief outline, was the tenor of the early Christian gospel, and explains why they were not interested purely in ethics, but in religion and salvation. The imitation of the sinless, patient and forgiving life of Jesus Christ was meaningless without the gospel of power whereby man could live such a life. They preached Jesus Christ, the power of God unto salvation.

It may be interesting to inquire what kind of a spiritual journey these Christians travelled before they came to know this gospel of the divine life and power. One early Christian of a philosophical turn of mind, Justin Martyr, has left us an account of his spiritual history and his case cannot have been unique. He tells of his interest in philosophy, not as an idle intellectual pastime, but as a serious way of life, and how he went to a Stoic to get some knowledge of God. He spent a considerable amount of time with him, and only left when the Stoic failed to give him any real knowledge of God, deeming such instruction unnecessary. He then went to a Peripatetic who fancied himself shrewd. This master appeared to be more interested in settling the fees for instruction than imparting knowledge to his pupil, so Justin sought another tutor. He then became acquainted with a very learned Pythagorean who had quite a high estimate of his own wisdom. After an interview in which Justin expressed his desire to become his pupil the philosopher asked, "Are you acquainted with music, astronomy, and geometry?" He impressed upon him the long course of intellectual preparation necessary in order to "perceive those things that conduce to a happy life." Justin had to confess his ignorance of these branches of knowledge and rather impatiently left him. In his helpless condition, for the search for the true way of life was a serious matter with him, he turned to the Platonists, who then enjoyed great fame. One of them in his own city had a high reputation and from him Justin learned much. "The contemplation of ideas," he says, "furnished my mind with wings." But even here he was fated to be disappointed. Certain and serious knowledge of God was withheld from him.

During this period of religious uncertainty he used to wander alone by the sea seeking quietness for his meditations. One day he met an old man and because of his striking and venerable appearance stared at him awhile. The old man was naturally embarrassed and asked, "Do you know me?" "No," replied Justin. "Then why do you stare at me so?" he inquired. Justin remarked he was astonished at finding any one in that desolate place. They then fell to talking of philosophy and the knowledge of God. The old man pointed out what fruitless attempts the philosophers had made to reach the knowledge forever hidden from them, and recounted how to the Hebrew prophets had been granted revelation or the direct knowledge of God. "They saw and announced the truth . . . they did not use demonstration in their treatises, saying that they were witnesses to the truth above all demonstration and worthy of belief." He then pointed to the fulfilment of the prophetic predictions and concluded, "But pray that above all things the gates of light may be opened to you; for these things cannot be perceived or understood by all, but only by the man to whom God and His Christ have imparted wisdom." This was the beginning of Justin's conversion, and although he never met the old man again, he was so concerned with what he had heard of the prophetic teaching that he set about studying it. He discovered that the words of the Saviour "possess a terrible power in themselves and are sufficient to inspire with awe those that turn aside from the path of rectitude." In Christianity he discovered that his earnest desire for salvation and for the knowledge of God was fulfilled.

The point of Justin's conversion has great significance for the modern day. Its emphasis upon the fact that man cannot reason himself into salvation and cannot be assured of the ultimate meaning of life by learning or by imagination needs to be recaptured. Any one who takes life seriously and knows the gravity of man's predicament in sin will not lightly consider that the knowledge of God is a matter of little moment. He will be driven to recognise that it cannot be deduced from reason and needs the authority of revelation. That is what Justin discovered in the teaching of the Church, which was the living witness to the revelation in the prophets and in Jesus Christ.

This revelation was of practical moment. It was not concerned with intellectual knowledge purely, but with life. It expressed itself in a community in which the revelation of God was preserved and made alive. The Christians were distinguished from the heathen, as Justin is constantly making plain, not only by their ideas but by their life and worship. Of the purity of Christian life and the corporate nature of Christian worship Justin has much to say. From his pen we have the first definite account of early Christian worship and the full meaning of his teaching can only be grasped in its relation to Christian life. It is an erroneous interpretation of Justin to imagine that his Christianity was purely concerned with intellectual knowledge of the divine.

For him the revelation in Christ is something of more momentous importance. It deals with the vital and ultimate meaning of life. It gives us the authority by which we know who God is and what His demands upon us are. Christ, he says, was no sophist, for His utterances had in them the power of God. For him the gospel of Christ was salvation from death and sin. Justin fully recognised the inability of man to know the divine law and he stressed the necessity of the incarnation of the Divine Word, because man's disobedience and the consequent corruption of his nature made him incapable of living the life ordained for him by God. It is true that Justin, in common with the Greek point of view, thought of salvation in terms of redemption from ignorance and restoration to truth, but these terms must not hide from us the inner meaning of his Christian outlook. To him there was a strength, a mightiness, in the gospel of Christ, which saved men from the false gods to whom they were formerly enslaved. Only in Christ could men know with assurance what was the will of God for them and in Him alone was to be found the power by which men could overcome evil. To live according to the Word in Justin does not mean to live rationally, in the sense of the eighteenth-century Enlightenment. It is not living according to the generally accepted precepts of men but according to the plan of God, which all men may vaguely apprehend by the light of reason and conscience, but which is fully grasped only in belief in the Incarnation.

This gospel of the divine life and power was embodied in a community, a people. It was a fellowship founded upon faith and ruled over by the abiding spirit of Christ. In order to appreciate fully the meaning of this community it will be our purpose to consider it from outside, as well as from inside. We shall ask what the educated pagan, as well as what the early believer, thought of this Christian fellowship.

THE PAGAN LOOKS AT THE CHURCH

The Ultimate Loyalty of the Church: Christ or Cæsar

The early Christians aroused the contempt of the cultivated pagan. They appeared to be an obstinate and unsocial people, recruited mostly from the uneducated classes and making for themselves quite outrageous claims. That is the picture we have from Celsus and other opponents of the early Christians. They were obstinate, because they would not worship the Emperor, and so confess that the ultimate meaning of life was the order and civilisation of the Roman Empire. It did not entail the belief that the Emperors were personally gods. No Roman anywhere near Rome really thought that. Close association with various Emperors could easily dispel such illusions. What was at stake was the conflict of two meanings of life. Just as Fascists and Communists nowadays believe that social and political organisation is life's ultimate meaning, so did the Romans. The Emperor was the symbol of the divine power in the Empire which was summed up and unified in him. This the early Christians clearly saw, and the conflict of Christ and Cæsar was very real. Modern people often wonder why the Christians refused to sacrifice to the genius of the Emperor. After all, to the Roman this meant little more than saluting the flag means to us. It was just a sign of patriotism and plenty of Romans who held a variety of private religious opinions and belonged to different cults were willing to do it. But precisely there lay the central issue. The pagan Roman had many gods, his private ones as well as the public Roman deities and the genius of the Emperor. To him there was no conflict between them. Perhaps he vaguely imagined these gods were united in some transcendent sphere, in a kind of philosophical monism. He was not unwilling to give a religious significance to the divine power in the Empire, for to him the civilisation and culture and peace of Rome did in some way represent the ultimate meaning of life. This the early Christian refused to recognise, just as the modern Church in Germany refuses to surround the Nazi State with a divine halo and to believe there is any ultimate and divine significance in the race and blood and culture of Germany. The Christian would thus rather suffer anything than deny his God. Christ and Cæsar were mutually exclusive. The divine life was not evident in the culture and peace of the world, but was only made Man and Incarnate in Jesus Christ. The Empire with all that was admirable and just in its culture and law was human: to call it divine was blasphemy. The Emperor could not give the Christian the kind of salvation that he had found in Christ.

Thus the claims of Cæsar and Christ seriously conflicted and the struggle between them was made all the more acute by the fact that the same terms were applied to both. In Asia Minor, for instance, Cæsar was hailed as *Soter* (Saviour), because the imperial régime, with the *principatus* system, had enormously benefited the Asiatic provinces, releasing them from the burdens of financial corruption and extortion, which had been imposed by the greedy officials of the old republican era. The benefits that the Empire derived from the Cæsars were often very significant, but they were always material and cultural. While the Romans could and did regard these as of ultimate meaning and divine, to the Christian they were transitory, earthly and human. They might in some sense be the gifts of God, but they could never in themselves be divine.

This firm faith naturally appeared to the cultured heathen as plain and downright obstinacy. When the Empire was struggling to maintain itself in a grave internal crisis, by transforming the old republican structure into a semi-oriental despotism and founding its basic unity upon a divine sanction, the Christians were creating unpatriotic trouble by refusing to "salute the flag." The pagan could not appreciate the religious issue from the Christian point of view, because he did not believe that divine and human were by nature essentially different, and that man and all his material and cultural world stood before his Creator as condemned and yearning for salvation.

To appreciate fully these conflicting claims, let us transport ourselves to the Roman courtroom in Scili in North Africa where we can watch a Christian trial in progress. By a fortuitous circumstance the court record has been preserved. It is the 17th of July, 180 A.D.,[1] and six Christians are up for trial before the proconsul Saturninus. He advises the stubborn Christians that they can easily get the indulgence of the Emperor if only they return to sanity. Speratus, the spokesman of the Christian group, replies that they have never done wrong and have always paid proper respect to the Emperor. He adds that he is willing to tell the proconsul the "mystery of simplicity" if he will only listen in good temper. This Saturninus refuses to do, saying that the Christians will speak evil of what is most sacred to the Roman, the genius of his lord, the Emperor. Speratus then renounces "the Empire of this world," and claims to serve God. He says he has committed no theft and always paid the legal sales tax, thus implying he is being unjustly accused by the court of wrongdoing.

To cut the argument short Saturninus says, "Give up your religion and don't be a fool." Speratus replies that it is a bad religion to do murder and utter false witness. By this he seems to mean that emperor worship implies the worship of war and that any denial of Christianity he might outwardly make would be an untrue testimony. Several of the other Christians now speak. Cittinus says, "We have none to fear save God in heaven." Donata adds, "Honour Cæsar as Cæsar, but fear God." These brief ejaculations go right to the point. They clearly reveal the central dilemma of Christ or Cæsar in the Christian mind.

---

[1]During the reign of Commodus. It must be remembered, however, that Christian persecution was for the most part local and intermittent before the first really severe attack on the church by Decius in 249. The ill success of this and later persecutions was not a little due to the fact that the first really concerted and centralised effort to stamp out Christianity came after the Church had had two centuries in which to develop a mature ecclesiastical organisation.

Saturninus then asks, "Do you still persist in being a Christian?" Speratus and all rejoin, "I am a Christian." The proconsul bids them take time to think the matter over. Speratus aptly replies— and this is absolutely basic for the faith of the Early Church— "There's no need for consideration in so straightforward a matter." The Christian point of view is simple and obvious. Saturninus then asks what they have in their box, apparently charging them with magic. "Some books and letters of Paul, a good man," Speratus simply replies. Again Saturninus bids them take a month to think their position over. They all insist they are Christians and will remain so. The proconsul then reads the decree. Since they persist in their faith after a chance to recant has been offered them, they are to be put to the sword. Speratus cries, "We give thanks to God," to which Nartzalus adds, "Today we are martyrs in heaven." The herald then reads the declaration and they are led out to be executed.

The simple dignity of this account needs no words of further explanation. The Christian saw with clear vision what the worship of Cæsar meant and the kind tolerance of the proconsul was of no avail. To him Christians were unpatriotic idiots, to them he was an unbeliever who neither saw nor understood the "mystery of simplicity." So is it always with the Christian faith.

Christian Life in the Church

To the pagan the Christian also appeared to be anti-social. He would not participate in the festivals of the time with their debauchery and paganism; he refused to join the army, not only because military service entailed the duty of sacrificing regularly to the Emperor, but because he regarded bloodshed as unchristian. He held aloof from the stage with its immoral life, from prostitution, and from such trades as those of goldsmiths, silversmiths, and painters, when they entailed making idols. Augury, magic, and astrology with their pagan associations were equally forbidden to Christian converts. This discipline the Church authorities imposed with rigour and general consistency. It greatly contrasts with the lack of such measures in the Church today, where we find Christians participating in trades and business practices which outrage the Christian conscience.

The Christian communities did at times arouse the praise of the heathen world. Their extensive system of charity, which often cared for the poor heathen as well as for the deprived Christian, provoked the admiration of the pagan Emperor, Julian. The goodness and gentle humility of the Christians was satirised by Lucian, whose hero, Peregrinus, was wise enough to prey upon their kindness and made quite an income out of these apparent simpletons. Yet the pure moral life and high conduct of the Christian did not pass unnoticed or without the admiration, and even the jealousy, of the pagan world.

An interesting picture of Christian life is reflected in the Apology of Tertullian (late second century). He first disposes of the various calumnies brought against Christians, such as adultery and the eating of new-born infants; immoralities imagined by the heathen mind because the Christian Eucharist was always held in secret and only believers were allowed to be present. He then shows that Christians do not even indulge in the general social practices, as the immodesty of the theatre or the cruelties of the arena.[2] They do not get themselves drunk at the wild festive parties nor squander their means on feasts or drinking bouts. Unlike Roman fathers they consider it wrong

[2]Christians also avoided heathen law courts to settle differences that arose between them. When such an issue came up it was the custom for the bishops with other clergy to hold a kind of Christian court on a Monday and judge the matter with impartiality, striving to maintain Christian love and friendship among the disputants.

to expose infants, leaving them to the mercy of some compassionate passerby who may take them up. In short, the Christian society is a body knit together by a common religious faith and by a unity of discipline. They take seriously to heart the commandments of God, and at their worship there are frequent exhortations to the good life and rebukes against sin. They have a treasure chest in the community and the members make voluntary contributions each month. The proceeds are not lavished on feasts and elaborate banquets (the general custom of the heathen guilds), but the money goes to support poor people, to provide the wants of destitute boys and girls, to assist aged people who are unable to work and to help those who have suffered shipwreck (a considerable body of needy people in the Roman world). The Christian community has one mind and soul—it shares its earthly goods no less than its spiritual treasures. "We have everything in common," Tertullian writes, "except our wives."

This picture of the Christian fellowship is doubtless idyllic and, written as it is for an apologetic purpose, it naturally tends to describe Christian conduct at its best. Yet the general tenor of the Christian life was such that the heathen could not but admire its moral earnestness and its liberal charity. The effect of Christian ideals upon the later Roman civilisation cannot be overestimated, and while after the recognition of the Faith by Constantine the general high level of Christian conduct was greatly lowered, Christian morality played a very significant rôle in advancing social legislation and in gradually reducing slavery. The effect in the West was particularly marked where the whole social system of Feudalism, which will occupy our attention later, was given a Christian interpretation. In the East Christianity had to contend with an alien tradition and culture in which

Hellenic and Oriental elements were blended and hence its effects were more limited than in the West. There the barbarian invasions and the distintegration of the Empire provided the opportunity for the development of a more independent and creative Christian culture.

THE CHRISTIAN IDEA OF THE CHURCH

Ekklesia

What did the Christians think of their own community, and what claims did they make about the nature and purpose of the Church? There were a number of words and metaphors used by the Christians to describe their community and each added something to their concept of the nature of the corporate life in Christ. The first word they seem to have appropriated was "Church," a term which had had a long history before the Christians used it in their peculiar sense. Our English word "Church" is derived from the Greek *ekklesia*, a common classical word for an assembly and often used in the technical sense of a body of citizens summoned by the herald. It is the Hebrew background of the word, however, that was determinative for the Early Church. In later Judaism there were two terms used of the people of Israel. One signified the local congregation of Jews in any given place (synagogue); the other meant the ideal Israel, the whole body of those who had been called by God to salvation. It was this latter Hebrew term which was translated by the Greek *ekklesia*, and in this particular sense it was used by the Christians. They regarded themselves as the true Israel, the remnant which was faithful and had been called by God. The other Jewish word (synagogue) appears very infrequently in Christian literature. Probably it was purposely avoided by the

Christians to distinguish their communities from those of the Jews. It is, of course, a platitude to say that the primitive Christians were mostly Jews. To the outside world they appeared to be a party within the Jewish Church, but the intrinsic distinction soon became evident and the rift was not long in developing. The Christians claimed to be the true Israel and the inheritors of the promises made by God to Abraham. The rigid racial bounds that encircled Judaism were burst asunder and the New Covenant, which God had made through the sending of His Messiah, was set in contrast to the Old Covenant which it superseded. He whom the prophets had foretold had come, and salvation from sin was accomplished for all who truly believed on Him. The Messiah had actually done what the old sacrificial system, as a means of forgiveness of sin, had merely foreshadowed.

By the term "Church," then, was meant the one body of the faithful called by God, the unity of the New Israel. Only in a secondary and derivative sense could the word be used in the plural to signify the local Christian communities, a use that was doubtless influenced by the pagan connotation of the same Greek word. The early Christians started with an awareness of the unity of the whole people of God, of which the individual congregations were but the representative and local manifestations. The fundamental distinction between Christians and Jews was the belief that the Messiah had come and that the new age foretold by the prophets and looked for as some distant future event by the writers of the apocalyptic literature, had actually begun. God's rule was no longer a purely future hope, but was a real and present experience. Its full consummation, indeed, had yet to be revealed, and so the faith of the primitive Church was firmly fixed on the immediate return of Christ in glory. Nevertheless, this approaching completion of history would be nothing else than a heightening of the present reality of the rule of God in men's hearts, which had been ushered in by Christ, the Messiah. As the writer of the Epistle to the Ephesians (1:14) put it, the Christians had received through the Holy Spirit a sample, an installment, of their inheritance, and were awaiting the complete legacy which would be theirs when God brought in the Kingdom.

The Christians did not regard the Church as an institution; rather was it that corporate body of God's people, who by faith had accepted His rule and recognised His Messiah. Under the control of the Spirit of Christ, they were living in the New Age, waiting for its consummation, but nonetheless conscious of it as a present experience. The time was fulfilled; the new age had come; these were the watchwords of the early Christian gospel. The Church, for them, was essentially the fellowship of the new age.

By the use of this term *ekklesia* they implied that they were a people chosen and called by God, and bound together with ties far deeper than those of family or race. Never was the sense of corporate life more perfectly felt and expressed than in these early believers. They were one people united in a bond of supernatural love and in a relationship of mutual dependence, mercy and forgiveness. This was impossible on a purely human level and was only realised in Christian life, because it was the direct gift of God through Jesus Christ.

This contrast between the natural relationships of the world and the divine fellowship of the Church finds frequent expression in Early Christian literature. Christians are pilgrims, sojourners in the world, waiting for the consummation of history. Their true citizenship is in heaven. The word "parish," when applied to Christian communities, had this meaning. The Greek term originally signified the inhabitants of a town, who did not have full civil rights, and it was also referred to the colonies of the Jews who were nationally distinct from the rest of the citizens. In a similar way it was used by the Christians. Though they dwelt in the world, their eyes were fixed on a more abiding City. The Church in Smyrna, for instance, addresses a letter "to all the 'parishes' of the Holy Catholic Church everywhere."

The Body of Christ

The sense of the mutual dependence of Christians upon each other gave rise to another term by which their community was described—the Body of Christ. The word "body" in classical Greek was never used of a community sharing a corporate life, but the equivalent Latin word had the technical sense of corporation. This idea was further deepened by the Stoic philosophy, with its concept of the unity of all mankind sharing in the divine Reason. Philosophers like Epictetus often used the figure of speech, by which individual men were regarded as members of one another, sharing in common the divine Reason. Some of these ideas passed into the later Greek use of the word "body," and Philo used it as a simile for the unity of the people of Israel. It was at this period that the Christian Church adopted it, first through Saint Paul.

He thought of the Christians as one people called by God to salvation and sharing in this new divine life of love. Nothing could more admirably express this sense of unity and mutual dependence than the Greek word "body" with its past history. But it is to be noted that Paul gave the term an altogether new sense. When he talked of the Body of Christ he did not think of corporate life on its purely natural and human level; he meant the new, divine life of mutual love and forgiveness, which had been made possible only through Christ's removing the obstacle of sin. Furthermore, the Christians were not just a body; they were one body *in Christ*. The word has an upward reference of supreme importance. The love which makes the Christian community a body is the Divine Love which comes from God; it is the love which is only realised by being in Christ—under His control, dominated by His Spirit, confessing Him as Saviour and Lord. The metaphor is further developed by Paul when he speaks of Christ as the Head of the Church. The underlying concept is the complete dependence of the Christian community upon Christ, who guides, rules, and directs it, and to whose control the Church is ever submissive.

The most profound thought of Paul in this connection is the relation of this body of Christians in Christ, to the Eucharist. It is difficult to appreciate this idea of Paul, since the united life of the Christian community no longer centres for many around the Table of Our Lord. Up to the Reformation no Christian could conceive of the basic and central service of Christian worship as anything else than the Eucharist. Just as the rite of Baptism initiated men into the Christian community, so the sacrament of the Lord's Supper was the continuation of the life of Christ in the Church.

The Eucharist

In its origin the Eucharist was a common meal that Christians shared, but it had a deeply religious significance. The word *agape,* which expressed the new life of divine love in the community, became a technical term for this supper. Around it there centred a wealth of association and religious truth.

It was regarded as the continuation of the meals that Christ had shared with His disciples and it derived even more profound significance from the experiences of the Risen Christ, many of which had been consummated with table fellowship. Religious joy was the predominant emphasis of this early worship—a joy rooted in the Resurrection and the hope of the immediate return of Christ in glory. But in this table fellowship there was also a more solemn element which was especially stressed by Saint Paul. The religious meals of the disciples looked back to the Last Supper of Jesus on earth and to His act in sharing with them the bread and wine, by which He had symbolised that He would give His life for the sake of the world. He believed that His impending death would in some sense inaugurate the Kingdom, the rule of God among men. So the Eucharist[3] was a commemoration of the sacrifice of Christ. Furthermore, linked with the expectation of the coming Kingdom which had marked the words of Jesus at the Last Supper (Luke 22:18), there was in early Christian worship both a vivid sense that the rule of God had begun and also a firm hope that this divine rule would be consummated and made perfect in the immediate future.

Precisely at what moment in these meals of the primitive Church the sacramental bread and wine were shared is hard to determine. It probably came at the close and was marked by prayers which set the elements apart and by a final thanksgiving after they had been distributed.

One of the earliest descriptions of Christian worship has been preserved in the *Apology* of Justin Martyr (middle of the second century). The account he gives is direct and simple, and he avoids technical terms, since he is writing for the heathen. The service, which takes place on a Sunday, starts with the reading from the Old Testament prophets or from the Gospels (which

[3]Literally, "thanksgiving," a technical term for the early Christian service.

Justin calls "Memoirs of the Apostles"). This is followed by a simple sermon from the minister (Justin calls him "The President"), who exhorts the congregation to live up to their profession of Christianity. Then they all rise and an extempore prayer of intercession is said. The Kiss of Peace, symbolic of the true fellowship of the early Christian community, is given. The bread and wine are collected by the deacons, and the minister mixes the wine with water. Another extempore prayer is said at length by the minister. It is a prayer of thanksgiving, and includes the account of the Last Supper with the traditional words that Christ said over the bread and wine. At its conclusion the people all give their assent by saying "Amen." The elements are then administered and the deacons take away portions for the sick and for others who could not attend.

From this simple account of Justin it is clear that the Eucharist as a religious rite by itself has become dissociated from the table fellowship of the primitive Church. Precisely when and why this happened it is impossible to say. It may have been due to the fact that religious clubs were strictly supervised by the Roman Government and meals of fellowship were frequently forbidden on political grounds. Such clubs often met to foment rebellion and to disturb the peace of the Empire. Christianity, as we have seen, was early regarded as a disloyal and unpatriotic movement aimed at destroying the foundations of the Roman Government. Not a little was this impression heightened by the somewhat reckless and fervent apocalyptic dreams of early Christians, who talked about Christ the King and regarded the coming of their kingdom and the destruction of Rome as events of the very near future.

The Eucharist, then, became separated from the original table fellowship, but the communal meal which retained the name of

Agape, or Love Feast, was not entirely discontinued. We have accounts of it in Tertullian, and it seems to have played some rôle in the West down to the early fifth century. Such meals were often given by private Christians in their homes and later on they were held as memorial feasts for the martyrs. Disorderly conduct was often their besetting sin, as it had been in the days of Saint Paul (I Cor. 11:22). Indeed the final suppression of the *Agapai* was due to the fact that they frequently became occasions for lavish banquets rather than for religious ceremonies. They were associated with heathen rites such as the *Parentalia,* and feasting and debauchery became the order of the day. Thus the canons of Laodicea (in the middle of the fourth century) and of successive Councils forbade them altogether.

The full significance of the Lord's Supper in the Early Church was by no means exhausted with the idea of a feast of commemoration. Just as Christ at the Last Supper with His disciples had taken the bread and wine to symbolise His own Body and Blood given for the world, so at the Christian Eucharist these elements took on the inner religious meaning of the whole Christian gospel. They became not symbols only, but a sacrament.

The problem of the nature of a sacrament, which has particularly agitated the Church since the days of the Reformation, can hardly be compressed into a paragraph. It must suffice to point out that any attempt to discover the meaning of the sacramental language of the Early Church must avoid two extremes. The actual physical constituents of bread and wine can neither be identified with, nor divorced from, the divine energy which they are seen to convey. The former position leads to superstition and magic; the latter fails to penetrate to the heart of the problem. Through the Christian tradition the sacramental elements have been indissolubly connected with the experience of renewing the divine life in the Christian community. They are more than symbols, not only because of the profound associations that have hallowed them, but because Christians have there experienced the power of God. In the deepest moment of religious insight the mere physical substances disappear, so to say, and the communion of man with God transcends all earthly limitations. On leaving the sanctuary the believer finds these same elements reassert themselves in their physical reality of bread and wine; yet they have been more than bread and wine, more than mere symbols of Christ's Last Supper. They have brought the very life of God.

This idea lies behind the words of Paul, when he speaks of the bread and wine as the Body and Blood of Christ. The very energy of God which has been made available for man through Jesus Christ, His Body and Blood, His life and sufferings, is constantly granted to him for the nourishment of his whole being in this sacrament of the Christian community. There the oneness of the Church is made most evident, when the faithful feed together on the life of God which has been poured out for them in the Incarnation and in the continuity of that life in Christ, which is to be found in the Church.

It is not surprising, therefore, that we find in Paul a twofold use of the term "body," when referred to Christ. On the one hand, it is a metaphor for the interdependence of the Christian community. They are severally the members of one body, the head of which is Christ, its leader and guide. On the other hand the word refers to the Incarnation, to Christ's assumption of a human body in order to bring the divine life to man. The close association of these two ideas is of great importance. It is essentially in the act of the sacrament that the unity of the whole

Church, beyond the limits of space and time, is realised, and the interdependence of each member of the community upon the other is most acutely felt. But this is not all. The sacrament entails the act of devotion, which recognises the divine source of this life in the community. God Himself, through the Incarnation of His Son and by His Spirit, has poured out the divine life on believers and made it possible for them to renew it in the sacrament of the Body and Blood of Christ.

The whole emphasis of the early Christians was upon the divine source and corporate nature of the Christian faith. They knew nothing of individualistic Christianity; they could not think of their belief apart from the Church. They prayed, as Christ had taught them, *our* Father, never *my* Father. Their practice reflected this conviction. The richer churches helped the poorer churches; the more fortunate members gave liberally to aid their less privileged brethren. The nature of this early Christian "communism" must not be misunderstood. It was a liberal, sincere, and spontaneous outburst of Christian charity; it was not an economy planned for the long future. The fervour of their new faith and their belief that the end of history was near at hand and that God would bring in His Kingdom very shortly, prevented their preoccupation with worldly affairs. The liberal bestowal of their property was a secondary and spontaneous matter.[4] Nothing was further from their thoughts than that an

---

[4]The community at Jerusalem was notoriously poverty-stricken and even received aid from the Asiatic churches. It was the practice of the Church during the first and second centuries to aid those in need. When the Church began to grow in numbers and in rich members, the situation changed, and constant exhortations to liberal alms-giving became necessary. One of Cyprian's treatises (written in the middle of the third century) reflects a generation, where the wealthy were most indifferent to the distress of their poorer Christian brethren. However, the Church was not vitally concerned with the problem of wealth till the period after Constantine. Then, as in modern times, the Church enjoyed some popularity. Good preaching was to be heard, and the rich callously disregarded the needs of their poorer Christian brethren.

equal distribution of their goods would be "extending the Kingdom." It was God and not man who would bring in the Kingdom, and the Kingdom would be not of this world. It would be the complete rule and dominion of God, a foretaste of which they now enjoyed in their united fellowship with Christ and with the Church.

What, then, did the Early Church conceive as its primary function? It was nothing else than witnessing to the gospel of Jesus Christ and renewing the divine life, by worship and service in the Christian brotherhood. In whatever station of life Christians were, slave or free, they felt themselves to be in the world, but not of the world. They had tasted the salvation of God and little else about earthly circumstances mattered, save the spreading of that gospel and the work and worship of God in the life of the Christian community.

The close connection of work and worship clearly appears in a consideration of the place of the offering in Early Christian liturgy. This offering was of a two-fold nature. It was, first, the corporate act of Christian devotion, whereby the faithful offered "themselves, their souls and bodies" to be a "living sacrifice unto God." At every Eucharist they dedicated themselves to God and renewed their life in the power of the gospel. Intimately connected with this was the offering or sacrifice of "praise and thanksgiving." Unlike the heathen, they did not sacrifice the blood of animals, but the purer sacrifice of themselves and of their prayers they rendered to God.

The second type of offering devolved from this. It was the oblation of their gifts for the feast of the Eucharist and for their needy brethren. Each Christian brought some bread and wine and this was collected by the deacons and consecrated by the bishop or elders, so that the united offerings of the people became one sacrament. At the Eucharist they also gave freely of their substance[5] for the aid of shipwrecked sailors, orphans, widows, captives, and unemployed. All Christian brethren in need were cared for and nourished from this liberal treasury. Their corporate devotion and their practical life of love were knit together in a real unity. God in Christ was worshipped as the source of the divine life in the Christian community, and worship and work were known to be two aspects of one reality.

Sanctorum Communio

Another phrase closely associated with the idea of the Church in early Christianity is *Sanctorum Communio*. This is a term that was inserted late (about the fifth century) into the Apostles' Creed,[6] but one which expresses two ideas very early in the Christian tradition. The first use of the term signifies participation in holy things, and affirms the Christian conviction about the sacred things or elements in the sacrament. The meaning, however, which it bears in the Apostles' Creed, is that of fellowship with the saints. Although the origin of its late insertion in the Creed is obscure, the idea that the life of the Church transcends the bounds of space and time and that there is a real unity and fellowship to be enjoyed between the whole Church throughout the world and through the ages, is a very vital and early conception. The intercessory prayers which in every early Christian liturgy are associated with the canon[7] bear witness to the close relationship between the holy things of the Eucharist and the world-wide and timeless fellowship of all members of the Church of Christ.

[5] These included offerings in kind as well as in money, and early Christian prayers for the blessing of cheese, olives, and oil are still extant.

[6] Originally the baptismal formula of the Early Church in Rome.

[7] The central prayer of the Christian liturgy, during which the sacramental elements are consecrated.

Catholic

This is the idea that lies behind the original Christian use of the term "Catholic," or "universal." It refers to the essential unity of the whole Church, and is contrasted with the local congregation. This universality is regarded not only as the sum total of actual Christian communities, but as the transcendent unity of the people of God, of which the Church is uniquely aware in its worship. It is a qualitative as well as a quantitative concept.

In later generations the term "Catholic" came to bear the meaning of orthodox, and was used as the antithesis of "heretical." It defined the true Church to the exclusion of every other, and in contrast to heretical. So the martyr Pionius in the third century, when asked by the Roman magistrate at his trial, "To what church do you belong?" replied, "To the Catholic, there is none other in the sight of God."[8]

Succession from the Apostles

A further element to consider in the early idea of the Church is the succession from the Apostles (*Successio Apostolorum*) which has been a constant source of strife and trouble in modern efforts to unite the various churches. The idea first found explicit expression in connection with a schism in the Church of Corinth during the very early second century. It seems that some am-

[8]The modern use of the terms Catholic and Protestant is rather misleading. The original antithesis of Protestant was Papist, not Catholic, and the Reformers revived the original meaning of the word Catholic, which referred to the transcendent body of the people of God in contrast to the local congregation. In modern usage, however, the words Catholic and Protestant are contrasted in two distinct ways. Either they are used as antitheses, defining the opposition between the Roman Catholic Church and those communions that broke their allegiance with the Papacy at the Reformation; or else they are used as complementary terms, referring, on the one hand, to the thought and practice which is broadly characteristic of the Roman, Eastern Orthodox, and Anglican churches, and on the other to the Lutheran and Calvinist traditions. In this latter sense the terms are not mutually exclusive.

bitious young men had stirred up trouble and had tried to seize the reins of Church government by overthrowing their seniors, who were the properly appointed officers. When the news got to Rome, Clement the chief elder[9] of the Christians there, wrote in the name of the Church in Rome to this factious community, bidding them refrain from deposing their duly constituted ministers.[10]

He argued that these elders stood in the direct line of succession from the Apostles, who themselves appointed ministers in the new communities they formed. They added a proviso that when these should die, others should be duly set in their places, thus guaranteeing a direct line of descent. Clement does not say how these latter should be appointed, but they were probably elected by the consent of the whole community in Corinth and received their authority from other elders by the laying on of hands. This was originally a Jewish ritual which signified the transmission of authority to rule the local community and to interpret the Law.

What was the point of this direct line of succession? It was, first, to assure peace and unity in the life of the Church and to guard against faction and schism. These ministers, and there were several of them, ruled the community, had charge of

[9]The word "elder" is the English equivalent for the Greek "presbyter" and goes back to the ruling officials of the local Jewish communities. This government became the model for the early Christian Church, though it was soon adapted and radically changed.

[10]Clement does not write from the point of view that the bishop of Rome exercised a universal jurisdiction over the worldwide Christian community. This was a claim which was only later developed by the bishops of Rome and put forward first at the Council of Sardica in 343 A.D. The fact that Clement of Rome wrote to Corinth may be explained by the very close and somewhat unique relations of the two cities in social, economic, and political affairs. The attitude he adopts is one of brotherly admonition, resting his case upon the scriptures and upon examples drawn from the life of the Early Church. It may be noted that he writes in the name of the Church at Rome, does not distinguish between bishops and presbyters in his letter, and hints that authority ultimately rests not in the rulers, but in the consent of the whole Christian community.

Church finances, and presided at worship. Originally this latter function was probably, as in Judaism, open to all Christians with special gifts, or *charismata*. For convenience and order, however, presiding at worship soon became limited to the constituted rulers. As the ministry further developed, it passed into the hands of a single elder who was now called a bishop. It is generally assumed that this officer was originally a kind of chairman of the ruling elders. The practical exercise of authority in the community (the granting of letters of commendation and so on), and the expediency of having a single head, gradually paved the way for the limitation of the powers of the other elders, till their authority largely disappeared.

The second reason for insistence upon the duly constituted officers came a little later with the rise of heresy. To guard against schisms in the community it was necessary to have a single and living centre of authoritative teaching. This was most fittingly discovered in the ruling officers, particularly in the bishop. He, with the elders of the community, was regarded as the guarantor of orthodoxy, of the right teaching which had been handed down from the Apostles through the succession of Church officers.[11] Ordination entailed, as it did in the Jewish Sanhedrin, the authority to interpret the ancient teaching. The canon or rule of truth about the gospel, so necessary for the Church to preserve, was formulated into a definite creed. This was zealously guarded by those churches which could boast of apostolical foundation. Of these the foremost were Rome, Alexandria, Antioch, and Jerusalem. The lists of their bishops, claiming to reach back to the days of the Apostles, became the credentials of their right to define the truth of Christian teaching,

[11]In his famous work, written against heresies, Irenæus (bishop of Lyons, end of second century) particularly stressed this point.

which in unbroken succession had been handed down from the Apostles.

The third element in this apostolical succession appeared with the development of the idea of the ministry as a sacrificial order, corresponding to the Priests and Levites of the Old Testament.[12] With rather literal realism the Eucharist was interpreted as a re-enacting of the sacrifice of Christ on the Cross, and the Old Testament sacrificial analogies were pressed to an unwarranted limit. It was supposed, furthermore, that the bishop alone had the divine authority and power necessary to consecrate the sacrament.[13]

This further advanced the episcopal dignity. Indeed, it was against the bishops, as against the very bulwark of the Christian organisation, that the early persecuting edicts were especially directed. The bishops became not merely theoretically, but practically, the visible centre of the Christian Church.

During this period the bishop was always the bishop of the local congregation and the diocesan episcopate had not yet developed. That was a later growth which followed the dependence of the village and country churches on the towns, whence they had learned the gospel. This situation made it impossible for the

[12]This concept of the ministry developed out of the early Christian interpretation of the Eucharist as a sacrifice. Several ideas were involved in this. The elements were regarded as an offering to God. They were, for instance, a type of the offering of fine flour which, under the Jewish Law, was presented on behalf of those purified from leprosy. This was understood as symbolic of the Christian purification from sin by Christ. Furthermore, the true meaning of ritual sacrifice was interpreted by the Early Christians as prayer and thanksgiving. The Eucharist, therefore, could be regarded as a sacrifice especially pure and acceptable to God. A yet deeper significance was attached to this idea. The close association of the elements with the body and blood of Christ brought to the fore the remembrance of the sacrifice on Calvary. There Christ had achieved what the ancient bloody sacrifices could only foreshadow—the reconciliation of man with God. In the corporate worship of the Eucharist the Christians united themselves with this perfect offering of Christ for the sin of the world.

[13]The great exponent of this view was Cyprian, bishop of Carthage, in the middle of the third century.

bishop to preside at every eucharist and so this duty was entrusted to the elders. They took over the functions of leading worship and ruling in the local communities and so regained something of their original power, though they still came under the jurisdiction of the bishops.

Behind these various ideas which developed around the doctrine of apostolical succession lies something of great significance. The continuity of Christian life and teaching became so important, because the early Christians recognised that the gospel had a divine source in the Incarnation. It was not something that could be imagined and thought out by men; it not only entailed the preservation of the ethical teachings of Jesus but it comprehended in its most profound meaning the mediation of the divine life through an historical Church. Early Christianity was far from other-worldly. It was rooted and grounded in history. It was ever true to the conviction that, as God had sent His Son to become incarnate in Palestine, so the divine energy was mediated through the visible community of Christ on earth and particularly through the sacrament. Hence the continuity of that community, the historical succession of the divine life of love and of the teaching of salvation, were of supreme importance. Any one who takes seriously the historical reality of the Christian gospel will not idly brush aside the apostolical succession of the Church, in its original meaning, as of little significance.

In summary, then, we may say that the Church in the early days of Christianity was conscious of being a community called by God to salvation and uniquely bound together by the bonds of a love that was more than human, one indeed which had its source in God. The gospel which they confessed and to which they witnessed was one that affirmed God had come to man, and by the incarnation of His Son had revealed Himself and redeemed the corrupt nature of humanity. The worship of the Church was centred in the Gospel and the Eucharist, through which were mediated the power of God in Jesus Christ. Finally, while in daily life Christians still carried on the pursuits and trades of the world (though not without discrimination) and were liberal in their charity, their eyes were set upon the immediate coming of Christ in glory and the bringing in of the Kingdom, the end and fulfilment of history.

The question of the authority by which the Church in the early centuries believed it spoke can best be approached from a study of the prophetic outburst which came to be known as Montanism. This movement was born in Phrygia, in Asia Minor, and had about it that ecstatic quality characteristic of so much Oriental religion. It elevated the momentary visions of prophets to a primary place in religious truth, and its naïve confidence in the working of the Holy Spirit easily degenerated into the interpretation of human whims and fancies as the voice of God. Montanism, in its various forms, has constantly reappeared in the religious life of the Church. It was basic to much of the Anabaptist movement of the sixteenth century, and with a somewhat different emphasis is apparent in the "Buchmanites" today. The fact that it often comes so near the truth, re-emphasising the continuous and vitalising life of the Spirit of God in each member of the Christian community, makes it all the more dangerous. To distinguish between the voice of God in man, and man's setting himself up as the voice of God, is a task at once of the greatest moment and of the greatest difficulty. If in natural life the margin between genius and insanity is extremely hard to define, the difference between revelation and the deification of human impulses is even more precarious to gauge.

In its historical origins Montanism[14] was inspired by a passion for the most stringent morality and discipline in the Church. The Montanists were the Puritans of the early centuries, who opposed the laxity of their Christian generation with as much gloomy fanaticism as their successors of the Reformation. But the essential difference between their teaching and that of the Puritans, lay in the fact that the Montanists rested their case for the strictest morality upon the immediate promptings of the Spirit, whereas the later champions of this type of church life took the scriptures literally as their authority.

That the Montanist emphasis was sorely needed in its day can hardly be denied. The moral tone of the Church had been degenerating and the temporary loss of the faith, which fervently believed in the immediate return of Christ in glory, had led to a weakening of Christian enthusiasm which had its consequent moral results. It was during the persecutions under the Antonines (from the middle of the second century to the beginning of the third) that the Montanist fervour reached its height. Its belief in the age of the Paraclete (or Holy Spirit) and the near approach of the millennium when God would bring down the New Jerusalem, swept through Asia Minor and North Africa. The Montanist prophets and prophetesses broke out in the most frenzied utterances, claiming to have recovered the gift of speaking with tongues which had characterised the primitive Church.

Montanism, while rigidly orthodox in its basic creed, was the convinced opponent of that type of Christianity, which was learning to settle down in the world and was even making compromises with the general level of pagan life. The Montanist

[14]So-called from its founder, Montanus.

fervour expressed itself in opposition to all ecclesiastical Christianity and the zeal of its hope was intimately associated with a rigorous and ascetic character. The Montanists claimed to be the direct recipients of the Holy Spirit, who gave both the assurance of the near end of the age and the most minute regulations for Christian conduct and discipline.

The eloquent, gloomy, and rigorous lawyer Tertullian was most responsible for the spread of Montanism in the West. He was an interesting blend of the African and Roman temperaments; to a fiery and passionate nature he added a Puritanical legalism. Both these elements are clearly marked in his writings, nearly all of which are controversial. He disposes of his opponents with vigorous and eloquent sarcasm while demanding of the Christian the most ascetic and disciplined life. In his hands Montanism lost much of its wild ecstatic fervour, while its gloomy character was more emphasised. The laws he laid down for Christian conduct were minute in every detail and the sanction he gave for their authority was the direct voice of the Holy Spirit. He prohibited second marriages, held all mortal sins[15] committed after baptism to be unpardonable, though venial sins could gain forgiveness by the merit of the strictest penance. He forbade soldiers to wear chaplets of flowers, insisted on the veiling of virgins, condemned flight in persecution, and denounced all manner of luxury or ornament in clothing. Fasts and many other ascetic disciplines were demanded of the faithful, and Christian life tended to become even more severe and legalistic than under the old Judaic code.

In working out his position after his conversion to Montanism, Tertullian saw that the Church could no longer be defined by the constituted hierarchy, which the growing development of

15*I.e.,* idolatry, murder, and adultery.

the Church as an institution had emphasised.[16] Ordination and succession from the Apostles was not the authority of the true priest. The direct visitation of the Holy Spirit alone qualified a Christian to be teacher or minister. Thus the growing distinction between clergy and laity was renounced by Tertullian who taught that the priesthood was as universal as the Holy Spirit. The Church to him was the Church of the Spirit, not the Church which consists in a "battalion of bishops."

This attitude of Tertullian raises one of the most profound questions about the nature of the Christian Church and the authority of the Christian gospel. It is true that the laxity of Christian morals stands constantly in need of correction from those prophets whom God raises up to impress upon men the necessity of really living according to their Christian profession. Nevertheless, it is patent that the teaching and life of the Church can never ultimately depend upon the whims of any who claim to speak in God's name. This would bring nothing but untold confusion into the Christian gospel and would make the individual conscience the sole seat of authority. From time to time in Church history this is what has occurred and Montanists, Anabaptists, and "Buchmanites" have all advanced their extravagant claims to receive minute regulations for Christian life from the Holy Spirit and to know God's will in detail.

To guard against this resultant individualism the Church has claimed that it is the depository of the revelation of God, incarnate in Jesus Christ and witnessed to by the Apostles. Each generation of Christians has been forced to reinterpret for itself, in its own practical circumstances and culture, the revelation in Jesus Christ, and has believed that the Spirit of God has guided its efforts to understand and to live more completely the life which God has

16This was, however, Tertullian's view before he became a Montanist.

thus made possible. In general, the criterion and authority of the Church through the ages have been the Holy Scripture and the living and universal faith of the Church which has preserved an outward continuity with Jesus Christ and with the apostolic community.[17] Should we dispense with such criteria, imagining we have the word of God complete in ourselves, Christianity would be reduced to chaos. That is why the Early Church rejected Montanism, stressing the historical continuity of the ecclesiastical institution, which in its worship held to the one and undivided faith, and in its corporate life and thought tried to reinterpret it to successive generations.

THE CHURCH AND SINNERS

The Early Church was gravely concerned with the question of sins committed after baptism. This was not a purely speculative problem. Rather did it arise out of a very critical situation with which the Church found itself confronted during and after the persecutions. It raised a fundamental question about the practical Christian life. What kind of conduct is expected of those who belong to the Christian Church? On what terms can those who renounce their faith during persecution be readmitted?

We have already had occasion to mention that the lack of any sort of discipline in the Modern Church has deprived it of much of its vitality and has certainly made any concerted Christian action against the obvious evils of our world impossible. Our general conception of Church life nowadays is to attend services on Sunday and to live the ordinary life of pagan society during the week. We have lost the sense of the Church as a living com-

---

[17]This conception of the living and universal faith of the Church is aptly phrased by Vincent of Lerins in his famous dictum, *"Quod ubique, quod semper, quod ab omnibus creditum est."*

munity making demands upon us in every sphere of our daily life and work.

The problem of discipline in the Early Church falls into two sections. It concerns those sins which the Church visited with total excommunication and those which could be atoned for by a definite number of years of penance. In the latter case punishment inflicted by the Church was exclusion from the Eucharist for a period of years. The gravity of this will at once be realised when it is remembered what great significance was placed upon the Eucharist as the corporate act of Christian fellowship with God.

The problem gravely agitated the Church after the years of the Decian persecution (the middle of the third century), the first really concerted attempt by the Empire to stamp out Christianity. Many, fearing for their lives, lapsed into paganism, sacrificing to the Emperor. The state of the Church in Cyprian's day, during the long peace which had preceded the persecution, was certainly a dark one from the point of view of Christian morals. Laxity was the order of the day. Cyprian, the bishop of Carthage, gives many indications of this in his writing. He speaks, for instance, of the total lack of spirituality among the clergy as well as the laity. Bishops would devote most of their time to secular pursuits and hunt markets to advance their profits, while poorer Christians were starving. The clergy lent out money at exorbitant interest. Swearing was rife among Christians and marriages with the heathen abounded. Every art of luxury was practised. Women dyed their hair and painted their faces. Church quarrels were frequent. In short, the examples of the Apostles were altogether forgotten.

It is hardly surprising that a prophetic protest against this degradation of the Church should have arisen. It was equally to be expected that many professing Christians who took their faith so lightly should have denied it so quickly when their lives and property were at stake. When, however, the fires of persecution had momentarily ceased, the problem arose as to how to deal with these "lapsed" Christians, as they were called. A strict party, headed by the gloomy Novatian, demanded their complete exclusion from the Christian community, asserting that sin so heinous could never be forgiven in this world. A lax party, relying upon the lenience of "indulgences" granted by the Confessors,[18] stood at the opposite extreme, and would have instantly readmitted them passing over their former transgressions. It was, however, a middle party which eventually carried the day and the wisdom of its argument and practice has much to commend it.

One of its most prominent leaders was Cyprian, who, though at first inclined to the stricter party, struggled in his mind for a long while over the burning issue. After mature consideration he claimed that the Church had no right to keep from its communion those who were sincerely and truly repentant. Against the stringent Puritans he wrote, "Whereas the Lord left the ninety and nine . . . and sought after the one wandering and weary . . . not only do we not seek the lapsed but even drive them away when they come to us." Hence he would reinstate even those who had actually sacrificed as well as those who by bribery or lying had obtained certificates (*libelli*) from the magistrates, testifying to their patriotism. Yet in contrast to the very lax party, he contended that some sign of true repentance should be forthcoming from the lapsed and a system of appropriate discipline was introduced. Even those who had received certificates of in-

---

[18]The Confessors were those who had suffered torture or imprisonment for their faith. They were regarded by the Church with great veneration and, on the grounds of the merit of their sufferings, they claimed the right to grant certificates to the lapsed, demanding their instant readmission into the Church.

dulgence from the Confessors were required to undergo a period of penance. At first those who hàd actually sacrificed were not admitted to partake of the Eucharist till on their deathbed, but later the severity of this was reduced to public confession after penance.

The first important factor to recognise in this whole controversy and one that may surprise our liberal age is the fervent belief of the lapsed as well as of the faithful that reinstatement into the Church was a matter of the gravest moment for their salvation. The idea, so familiar to us, that joining the Church is of little ultimate significance and a kindly God will receive all decent living people into His care no matter how little they trouble about their faith, never entered the mind of the Early Church. These Christians were in deadly earnest: Christian life and the true confession of faith were to be taken seriously. Most of the lapsed recognised the enormity of their sin and for this reason they were so anxious to be reinstated into the Church.

The second thing to notice is that forgiveness must be preceded by true repentance. While the outward forms of penance may differ for our generation some system of discipline is necessary. Salvation in Christianity is not an automatic affair. It takes life seriously and believes that the confession of Christ and the entrance into the Christian community is of real and vital moment for eternal life.

A third consideration may be noted. The way in which Cyprian developed the doctrine of penance for sins committed after baptism led to the whole indulgence system of the Middle Ages. Instead of merely regarding penance as an outward sign of true and contrite repentance, he tended to look at it in much the same way as Tertullian. It is actual satisfaction rendered to God and stores up a definite amount of merit to compensate for the punishment incurred by the sin. This merit can be transferred to others in need of it,[19] though in the case of the lapsed Cyprian tried to guard against a too lax appropriation of the indulgences of the Confessors. Yet the whole doctrine of indulgence and merit when drawn out to its logical and practical conclusions vitally affected the course of Christian history and tended to neglect the profound belief of Paul that man must always rely upon the mercy of God in Christ and not on his own merit. It was this foundation truth of the gospel that Luther recovered at the Reformation.

A last factor, which will engage our attention further in the Donatist controversy, must also be mentioned. The Church constantly faced the danger of becoming a sect, defining its bounds by a rigid ethical code and believing that the gifts and graces of its membership depended upon the moral achievements of men. This would have transformed the Church into a man-made society, resting its claims upon its own merits. It would have denied the power of God who alone supports and sustains the Church and it would finally have led to the conclusion that the sacramental acts of the Church were dependent for their validity not upon the grace of God but upon the merit of man. Every attempt so to circumscribe the Church eventually falls into the glorification of men's moral attainments and issues in pride and complacency.

THE DEFINITION OF DOGMA

Christianity was a religion of salvation, dependent upon right thinking as well as upon right living. Hence it was that the Christian community had to make its position clear when rival interpretations of the gospel arose within its own circle. In these days

---

19A doctrine finally formulated in the Middle Ages as the "treasury of the Church," which the Pope alone could dispense by providing for the sale of indulgences.

of toleration, we are used to thinking that what a man believes is his own private affair and nothing much matters if he holds his convictions sincerely. Nothing could be further from the thought of the Early Church. It was of infinite moment for a man's salvation that he hold the right faith. This must be distinguished from philosophy. Doctrine is not arid intellectualism, a pastime of little significance, but it is an account of what we hold to be of vital and ultimate importance. The Church as a conscious witness of God's revelation in Jesus Christ was forced to defend its faith against rival faiths. That is what was really involved in the struggles against heresy. It was not a case of the Church fighting to maintain some particular philosophy. Rather was it life and death battle for its faith. What the Christian theologians tried to do was to show that the presuppositions of heretical positions were contrary to the fundamental tenet that God had become man in Jesus Christ. Although much of the Church's struggle against heresy does not reflect upon the good manners or Christian conduct of its protagonists, we must not blind ourselves to what was really involved in the controversies.

It is manifestly impossible for us to give an account of the whole development of the Church's thinking on the Incarnation, and of the various rival interpretations that it attempted to meet. It must suffice to take the examples of Paul of Samosata and the Council of Nicæa, in order to show what was involved in the debates.

There is no more interesting personality in the third century than Paul of Samosata and his condemnation gives us an opportunity to study not only the Church's thinking on the nature of Jesus Christ but also an element involved in most of the ecclesiastical controversies—Church intrigue.

We know comparatively little about this Paul of Samosata;

indeed, our information is almost wholly derived from the later
Church historian, Eusebius of Cæsarea. However, as this learned
writer was more a compiler than an original thinker we may give
fair credence to the documents he has embodied in his Church
History, where he gives us an account of this strange affair. It
appears that Paul was a man who cut something of a figure in
the Church of his day. He held a high political post in the government of Zenobia, Queen of Palmyra. At the same time he was
also Bishop of Antioch. It may be that his exalted position caused
not a little jealousy among other bishops. Anyway, reading between the lines of the synodal letter in which a number of them
condemned him and his views and excommunicated him from
the Church, it is evident that they were just as outraged by his
person and acts as by his theology. What had Paul done that
so annoyed his brethren? In the first place he had made innova-
tions in the Church service and had also become extremely
popular. He knew well how to play the demagogue in the Church,
where he built himself a lofty platform with a throne and had
a sort of secret office curtained off for private conferences, not
unlike the *secretum* of a civil magistrate. In his preaching he
would play up to the gallery, stamping on the floor and slapping
his thigh. He called for applause in his sermons and was delighted
when people waved their handkerchiefs and shouted and leapt
around with the enthusiasm characteristic of the circus. Then he
had a female choir, quite an. innovation for his day. Instead of
using the current hymns they sang special verses extolling him
and even claiming that he was an angel come down from heaven.
To this he added female companions who went about with him
and his clergy, arousing scandalous rumours in the neighbour-
hood. He had, it seems, succeeded in making himself a great
fortune which he neither inherited, being formerly rather poor,

nor accumulated through honest business, in which Church officers might be engaged during the week. He is supposed to have plundered those in difficulties by making them pay him sums of money in return for services which by the influence of his eminent political and social position he might be able to render. According to his enemies, however, he frequently deceived these panic-stricken people who were in trouble. Above all, he was reproached for being haughty and preferring to be addressed by a grand political title "Ducenarius" rather than as simple "Bishop." He would strut about the marketplace attended by a bodyguard and posing as a great and very important figure. Such was Paul of Samosata, the wealthy and swaggering demagogue who aroused the opposition of the neighbouring bishops.

What of his theology? He reintroduced a view of the nature of Jesus Christ[20] which had already been condemned and one which was, of course, not necessarily connected with Paul's character and worldly position. He held that Jesus was not the Son of God come down from heaven. Jesus Christ, he said, is from below. He was merely a good man who, because of his constant virtue and sinlessness, was gradually elevated to divine dignity, thus becoming the Saviour of the race. His moral rectitude showed that the Word of God dwelt in Him in greater measure than in any other mortal, but there was no radical difference between Him and the rest of men. He was not unique. His divinity was really the reward of His goodness and hence other good men can claim to be filled with similar divine power. Indeed, the accusation that Paul had hymns sung to himself, in which he was lauded as an angel come down from heaven, possibly arose from the central article of his creed, in which he held the divine power could be in all good men and hence in himself.

[20]Technically known as Adoptianism.

This is an extreme way of stating the general modernist position about the nature of Christ. Those who see Christ's divinity merely as the moral goodness of His character, who believe that He is essentially like other men except in the perfect rectitude of His life, miss the central factor of the Christian faith. It is not only Christ's likeness to men, but also His radical difference from them, that makes Him the Saviour of mankind. It is only because man in the predicament of his sinful nature cries out for salvation that the saving work of Christ has meaning. Christ as the good example which we can follow misses the deepest conviction of the Christian gospel. We cannot follow such a pattern of life unless in Him is the very power of God which redeems and restores our fallen nature and makes it possible for us to follow Him.

So it was that the Church condemned Paul of Samosata. Because of his great political influence, they had some difficulty in ousting him from the See of Antioch. The Emperor Aurelian finally interposed and, after referring the matter to the Roman and Italian Bishops, enforced the decision of the Synod of Antioch.

This case of Paul of Samosata well illustrates the position which the Early Church faced. It had to make decisions about the nature of the Christian belief and to show the false presuppositions upon which rival interpretations of Christianity rested. But it was not only in condemning and depriving heretics that the Church was engaged, there was also the positive task of stating what the true faith was. From this arose the need for some authority in the Church in order to prevent the gospel from becoming mere individual opinion and chaos.

The definition of dogma or correct belief is extremely difficult, as it stands constantly in danger of petrifying the vitality of Christian faith, and of reducing it to intellectual propositions to which assent is demanded. Furthermore, every interpretation of Christian belief involves some relative factors for which divine authority can hardly be claimed. The Church was thus faced with the problem of discovering the most practical way to reach conclusions about the intellectual content of the faith without falling into these errors. Their sense of the corporate nature of Christian life and teaching led them to use councils for the deliberation of these questions, as in the early days of the Church the leaders had met in Jerusalem over the question of circumcision (Acts 15). It was at such synods that Montanism, Novatianism, and Paul of Samosata had been condemned.

During the harassing years of persecution it was only practical to call local synods and conferences to settle these issues of heresy, though a relationship between these local councils and the wider Church was maintained through communications with the Apostolic Sees, which were regarded as the guardians of the apostolical tradition. When, however, Christianity was tolerated by the imperial power in the early fourth century, the calling of world-wide councils became possible; and thus the judgment of the whole Church represented by the bishops and other clergy was brought to bear on the issues at stake.

For the most part these early councils tried to condemn false interpretations of the gospel rather than to erect elaborate schemes of their own, fearing lest the relative element in all intellectual judgments should detract from the divine authority of the faith. Yet every creedal definition cannot escape the style of thought of its generation. From this arises the danger of identifying faith with our understanding of it. There were, however, two factors which constantly aided their efforts. Their sense of the Church as a world-wide community in Christ gave their decisions as broad a character as possible; while their firm hold on the unbroken continuity of the Church's life from the days of the Apostles gave their deliberations perspective and direction. We are today coming to realise the strength of this world-wide fellowship of the Church and the various modern ecumenical movements, though they lack the definitive authority of Church councils, are recapturing something of this spirit of the Early Church. Despite the differences of tradition, thought, and culture that divide the various communions, there is a growing sense of our spiritual kinship in Christ. To underestimate or disregard these differences would be to have a false conception of unity. But to attempt to understand them is our primary task. Christianity involves decision and is not characterised by that type of sentimental toleration which thinks there is no important distinction for Christian life between truth and error. The Early Church may not always have avoided the arrogance that thinks it knows all truth, but we stand in a far more dangerous predicament, if we think that no truth matters at all.

The first world-wide Christian council was held at Nicæa in the year 325 A.D. Such a gathering was only possible after the toleration of Christianity by the Emperor Constantine. Like former synods the Council of Nicæa was not only concerned with problems of heresy. Various regulations concerning the organisation of the Church and practical issues for Christian life and conduct, as for instance the question of the lapsed, had also to be considered. These problems, however, were more easily disposed of at Nicæa than was the momentous conflict with Arianism, the particular heresy which had caused the convening of the council.

The part played by the Emperor Constantine in this council must first concern us. We have already mentioned that the Empire in the second half of the third century faced a grave internal crisis. Civil war had been rife and military emperors had succeeded one another with unprecedented rapidity. The army made and unmade emperors: most of them reigned but a brief period of years and generally concluded their short-lived careers by being murdered. When Diocletian became the sole ruler of the Empire he saw clearly that a complete reorganisation was necessary. He removed the capital to the East, in order to be near what he considered the danger spot of the Empire, where the Persians were harassing the Eastern borders. Then he conceived the idea of creating a semi-Oriental despotism which would be a firm basis for a highly centralised government. He believed that this could only be achieved by severely limiting the powers of the Senate and by sweeping away the last vestiges of the old republican liberties. The state was thus saved at the cost of transforming the republican structure into an autocracy and at the expense of the freedom of the middle classes.

Finally, the unity of the Empire was given a fundamental religious sanction and the worship of the imperial genius received added and increasing emphasis. In large measure Diocletian's reorganisation succeeded; but in one particular, in the persecution of the Christians who refused this worship of the Emperor, he failed. Toward the conclusion of his life, worn out with the cares of the imperial administration and harassed by the deep rift that the Christian persecutions produced in the Empire, he retired from office. He is supposed to have remarked that he gained greater pleasure from cultivating cabbages in his garden than from ruling the Empire. It was the supreme contribution of Constantine to realise that the toleration of Christianity would solve the problem far better than would persecution. Indeed, behind Constantine's granting of material and religious privileges to the Christians there was probably the idea of making Christianity the sole religion of the Empire. When, therefore, Constantine found the Church itself divided in a schism over a theological question, which he neither understood nor thought was worth disputing, he did all he could to heal it. The peace he had attempted to establish by toleration was now endangered by the Church itself. He therefore devoted every effort to the settling of this issue. He doubtless believed that practical peace was of more consequence than theological precision.

After consultation with the Church authorities he decided on calling a council, and the imperial initiative here gave a precedent which the Church later regretted in its struggle over the extent of the secular power. In that day and generation, however, the Emperor's interest and action were the cause of universal Christian rejoicing. That he should show solicitude for the Church instead of persecuting it was a rare cause of thanksgiving. He invited the bishops of the Empire together with other clergy to attend a council in Nicæa, putting at their disposal all public conveyances and defraying the expenses of their journey from public funds. Some three hundred and eighteen bishops and some thousand presbyters and deacons came by the public post carriages or on horses and mules. The representation was mostly Eastern, though some from the farther provinces of the Empire were there.

The formal opening of the council is described by the first church historian, Euseþius of Cæsarea, who was an eyewitness. He tells with enthusiasm of the entrance of the Emperor, a man slender and handsome in appearance but with gravity and modest bearing. He was accompanied not by guards and soldiers but by friends in the faith. The brilliant splendour of his gold and purple robes contrasted with his downcast eyes and blushing countenance. When it is remembered that Eusebius had known the bitter years of the Diocletian persecution, it is not to be wondered at that he should have regarded Constantine as "some heavenly messenger of God." His account of the affair shows that he shared Constantine's desire to cement the peace of the Church as quickly as possible and arrive at a compromise rather than prolong the debate. He had little desire to reach decisions of too technical precision and was fearful of arousing the bitterness and animosity which such debates usually bring with them. His own position on the question was not too clear. He lacked the incisive insight of the great champion of orthodoxy at the council, Athanasius. He preferred a hazy theology and peace to a warfare of fine distinctions. Indeed, as we read Eusebius' account of the affair, we gather that he was more impressed by the great dinner that Constantine gave these ecclesiastics in honour of the twentieth year of his accession, than he was with the theological battle. Heresy was an old tale; but for an Emperor to give a dinner to Christians, instead of providing lions with a Christian dinner, was an astounding and unprecedented phenomenon. Looking round that dinner table Eusebius could see several who had suffered in the former persecutions. There was, for instance, Paphnutius, a bishop from Egypt, one of whose eyes had been put out, and Paul, bishop of Neo-Cæsarea, who had been tortured with red-hot irons and was crippled in both his hands. It is no wonder therefore that Eusebius grew eloquent in praise of Constantine, and thought the question of heresy of small significance beside this great reversal of the Church's fortunes.

Yet the heresy discussed in the prolonged debates had great significance. It was not a mere quibble over words: the basic doctrine of the Incarnation was at stake. The protagonist of the heretical party was a man Arius, a presbyter of Alexandria. He was past middle age, tall and thin, and he had a trick of twisting his body as he spoke. He had a wealth of learning, but was austere and disputatious in character. He claimed that there must be an essential distinction of essence or nature between Christ and God the Father. He thought of God the Father in the terms of Platonic philosophy, as One Wholly Transcendent, unknowable and incapable of having contact with our world. Jesus Christ stood in between man and God, as a mediating power or angel who could have contact with the world of sense and matter. Athanasius, the young arch-deacon of Alexandria, who had accompanied his bishop to the council, saw with incisive clarity whither this interpretation of Jesus Christ would lead. It would deny the very foundation of the Christian gospel that God Himself had taken action in history in Jesus Christ, who by the power of His divine nature had redeemed man and restored him to fellowship with God. Furthermore, this position of Arius involved a wrong understanding of God. The Christian faith asserted that God desired to bring back His wayward children and was not so wholly Other that He could not be known.

It was the lively eloquence and insistence of this young Athanasius—he was then scarcely twenty-five—that finally carried the day and stamped forever the orthodox understanding of the nature of Christ. In the definition of the dogma he insisted that Christ was "of the same nature" as God the Father. By this he did not mean to confuse Jesus Christ with God: but merely to assert, in unqualified terms, that the revelation of God in Christ was real. God was acting in history, reconciling man to Himself. Many at the council wanted to avoid any definition which brought in theological terms not found in Holy Scripture. Moreover, they felt such words were departing from the simplicity of the faith and only raised more and more difficult questions. But Athanasius stood his ground. He believed that any statement which was vague and did not explicitly deny the

teaching of Arius and affirm the Incarnation would not do justice to the Christian faith. The problem had been raised and it
had now to be answered with decisiveness and not with evasion.
The belief that God became man was so central and of such
vital moment that it must be guarded at all costs. The final
definition agreed upon was in the form of a creedal statement,
denying the position of Arius and affirming that the nature of
Christ was the same as that of God. This creed must not be confused with the so-called "Nicene Creed" in the Roman and
Anglican prayer books. The latter is a misnomer and had a
different history.[21] Arius and two of his followers who refused
to sign the creed were temporarily banished by Constantine,
though the conflict was far from ended. Arianism was by no
means dead after Nicæa and grew rather than diminished in
importance during the succeeding century. At one time it had
the ascendency in the Empire but finally was defeated.

The many problems raised by this definition of the nature of
Jesus Christ are beyond the scope of our book. The Council of
Nicæa was the beginning of a long controversy which reached
its conclusion only in the Council of Chalcedon in 451 A.D.,
where the affirmation that Christ is of divine and human nature,
fully God and fully man, and yet one person, was reached. What
it is important to notice in this Council of Nicæa is that the
essential belief of the Church that God had become man was
affirmed. The Incarnation as the central and basic doctrine of
Christianity was clearly asserted against the error of Arius.

[21]Originally this was a creed used in Jerusalem and in its present form is a
century later than Nicæa.

CHAPTER III

THE THINKING OF AUGUSTINE ON THE CHURCH
AND ITS POLITICAL BACKGROUND

AUGUSTINE'S IDEA OF THE CHURCH

WHEN the Church emerged at the beginning of the fourth century from its long conflict with the pagan state and began to enjoy the fruits of a lasting peace, an entirely new situation arose in Christian history. The hope of the immediate advent of Christ waned and the fires of fervent expectation, which had been fanned by each fresh persecution, were succeeded by a calmer and more sober outlook. The Church's life in the world was viewed in a longer perspective, and although the barbarian invasions of the West revived the belief in the approaching end of the world, the tenor of the Church's life and hope was changing. After the days of Constantine, the Church was firmly entrenched in the political and social culture of its day, and the pressing practical problems of this world, of the relation of ecclesiastical to other institutions, made the life of the Early Church an anachronism. The Church had a stake in this life; and, although the intermittent years of peace in the third century had often foreshadowed this development with its consequent moral corruption and religious compromise, it only reached its maturity in the period after Constantine.

The toleration of Christianity by Constantine can rightly be regarded as a turning point in the history of the Church. His successive edicts, at first allowing the existence of Christianity along with other religions and later granting it special privileges, brought to the fore two of the gravest problems with which the Church has since been faced. One of these concerns the relation of the Church to the State; the other has to do with the relation of the Church as an institution to salvation. Neither had been a pressing issue before. In practice and in theory the Church had stood in marked contrast to the persecuting State. It was by the voluntary act of faith, not by the command of the government, that Christians were united with the Church. The only possible relation of Church and State was one of bitter opposition and although the Christians deemed it right to pray for their rulers and to obey the secular government in every sphere but the religious, they imagined that the age was rapidly coming to an end. The laws and kingdoms of this world were but a transitory phase of existence, almost immediately to be swallowed up in the glory and dominion of God.

Furthermore, it cost something to belong to the Church. Life and property were constantly in danger, and it is generally true to say that Christians were sincere. The question did not arise whether all within the ecclesiastical institution were saved, because the distinction between the institution and the body of the faithful did not exist. The Church was the fellowship in Christ, the community of those who were called by God. In its outward life and practice it was a visible institution; but in its inner meaning it was the body of the faithful, the company of those who were saved.

It is true that the Montanists and Novatians tried to limit the true Church by strict moral bounds, but it is important to notice that they did not believe their laxer brethren were members of the Church at all. For them, as for the orthodox, the Church was essentially one, the body of the faithful who were saved.

No distinction between the saved and the institution had yet clearly arisen. For both parties the dictum "no salvation outside the Church" referred at once to the Church of the faithful and to the visible institution. The only issue concerned the precise delimitation of this single body of Christians.

The theologian who first clearly enunciated the doctrine that the visible Church in history could be distinguished from the true body of the faithful was Augustine. He was forced to his position by the Donatist controversy which was a burning issue in Hippo, the city where he was bishop.

The Donatists, following in the footsteps of the Montanists and Novatians, were anxious to raise the moral level of the Church of the fourth century and tried to exclude those who did not conform to a rigorous standard of discipline. The schism originated in their refusal to recognise Cæcilian as Bishop of Carthage.[1] They claimed he was a *traditor,* having given up the sacred scriptures to the Roman officials during the Diocletian persecution. On the grounds of the unworthiness of such a man as bishop, they denied that the so-called Catholic Church was the Church of Jesus Christ. They nicknamed it "the Church of Judas Iscariot," for they claimed that Cæcilian, like Judas, had betrayed his Lord. They contended that only their communities represented the true Church, since they alone were morally pure. The Catholics by the laxity of their standards excluded themselves from the true Church of God, which must ever be characterised by the strictest holiness. The Donatists claimed that the gifts and graces of the Church were dependent for their efficacy upon

[1]Many issues of internal jealousy among the clergy of North Africa were involved in this. Apparently Cæcilian was rather hastily elected and consecrated by the Carthaginians. The Numidian bishops, who previously had had a voice in the election of the Bishop of Carthage, were outraged by not being consulted. They, together with the disappointed Carthaginian candidates, formed the backbone of the disaffected party.

moral achievements; and the validity of the Church's teaching and its sacraments rested on the attainment of man. The logical result of this conception was to reverse the basic Christian belief. The power of Christ in the Church and in the sacraments was made to derive from man's moral virtue. The holy life, instead of resulting from the fellowship of the Church with God, was made its prerequisite.

Where this issue became of even graver consequence was in the doctrine of the ministry. The Donatists claimed that the personal virtue of the priest determined the value of his ministrations. The gospel he preached, the sacraments he administered, derived their efficacy from his moral character. The faithless priest could only minister faithlessness to his people, and hence those who received the sacraments would be in perpetual doubt of their validity. It was to correct this false notion, that man and not God is the measure of the Church and the source of its life, that Augustine developed his characteristic doctrine of the Church, which greatly influenced the future course of Christian thinking.

The contention of the Donatists to be the only true, pure, and holy Church, Augustine rebutted with a variety of arguments. He maintained that their schismatic act in breaking from the historic Church was enough to show that they lacked the most important virtue of Christianity, the gift of love or charity. Their divisive temper, he held, had cut them off from the channel of God's grace, which alone was to be discovered in the unity of the Catholic Church with its historical continuity. Thus the Donatists could not rightly claim to be the true Church at all.

In the course of the long debates with the Donatists, Augustine was forced to develop a position on the nature of the Church, which clearly distinguished the visible institution in history from the true body of the faithful. He conceived of the Church from two distinct points of view, which corresponded to the two basic aspects of his thought. He saw that two questions were really involved in a consideration of the nature of the Church. One might ask, "Who is saved?" and one might also ask, "How are we saved?" In thinking of the former his thought was controlled by the doctrine of predestination; in trying to answer the latter he was preoccupied with the concept of the Church as the institution through which God worked in the world.

The doctrine of predestination in Augustine must not be confused with determinism.[2] By it he simply meant that salvation is not something of man's own doing. It is an act of God. Man does not save himself. God bridges the gulf between Himself and man, giving him the gift of faith in Jesus Christ and enabling him to find reconciliation with his Creator. Predestination, then, is something very different from the later philosophical theory of determinism. To say that, since God saves or damns whom He will, there is nothing man can do about it, is to misconstrue the whole meaning of faith. He who realises the serious and impotent predicament in which man stands and who has known for himself the power of God unto salvation in Jesus Christ, is forced to say that it is God who has taken action in history; it is the Eternal who has broken into the temporal. He expresses this tremendous fact by saying that he is called of God, chosen, elect, predestined. In short, predestination is not a metaphysical theory, but a religious judgment; it is not concerned with answering the philosophical question of causation, it only gives expression to the deep insight that man's salvation is of God's doing and not his own.

From this point of view it would surely be presumption to imagine that we know all whom God has called, that we can

[2]In the sense that man's free will and moral responsibility before God are denied.

make rules by which accurately to test who are faithful and who are not. Yet this is precisely what the Donatists claimed to do. They imagined that, by the application of their ethical standards, they could discover what was known only to the infinite wisdom of God. There is no more tragic arrogance in the Church than that which denounces other people as unfaithful, because they do not measure up to our particular ideas of how a Christian should live and act.

To illustrate his position Augustine used the parable of Christ about the wheat and the tares. He interpreted it to mean that the elect and the non-elect were found together in the historic Church, but this was a situation which must continue to exist till the final judgment of God and the end of history. To try to weed out the tares was to assume to be God.

In reply the Donatists claimed that Augustine had two churches and thus had renounced the unity of the Church of God. Augustine, on the other hand, insisted that it was really one and the same Church, but its temporal manifestation must not be confused with its eternal nature. In its historic existence it was not yet perfect; it was now mixed with the ungodly but in its eternal fulfilment it would be pure and holy.

There is thus involved in Augustine's thought the conception of the Church as dynamic and not static. The Church on earth is always *in via,* it never fully attains. It is far from perfect and only at the advent of Christ and the end of history will it become what in germ it already is—the true people of God. The meaning of Christian history is "becoming," and not "being." The Church is increasingly realising God's purpose in the world but still has its warfare with sin and is not yet victorious. The ultimate meaning of history is the perfect and triumphant church which eternally "is," but in history this meaning is not yet fully realised:

the goal is not yet attained. In time there is only "becoming." In the historic Church there is hope, and not fulfilment.

The society of God upon earth can only be the inadequate, symbolic representation of the Eternal Kingdom. Yet these are two aspects of a single reality. The historic Church is the temporal manifestation of that which it will ultimately become. It looks in hope to the climax of history, but it knows that it has not yet attained. It is bound together on earth by a divine love, yet it is not completely at one with the Divine.

There was a second way in which Augustine regarded the Church. Not only could it be considered from the point of view of predestination, but it could be viewed as an instrument that God uses to make His purpose known unto men and to endow them with the divine life in Jesus Christ. Now, as a divine institution the Church in history had certain simple and objective marks by which it could be known. It had an apostolical foundation; it had a world-wide character; it had the sacraments which were the peculiar channels of God's grace; and it was knit together in unity. Such an institution had a tremendous appeal for Augustine. It is not an exaggeration to say that he was converted to the Church, rather than to a creed. The Church offered him the living faith and an unshaken authority that became for him, after long and weary philosophical wanderings, the haven in his quest for certitude. He found in it the divine act that answered the problem of scepticism, with which he had so long struggled. Its world-wide character he frequently dwelt upon. He contrasted it with the little heap of Donatists, who were confined to North Africa, a comparison which he emphasised the more, because the Donatists outnumbered the Catholics in Hippo.

The importance of this idea of the Church, as an institution possessing a divine life and authority, can only be grasped when we recall the circumstances of the early fifth century. The invasion of Rome by Alaric the Goth seemed to ring down the curtain upon the civilisation of the West. Men thought that the foundations of culture had been shaken and that the world was being enveloped in a nightmare of chaos and destruction.[3] Rome, the Eternal City that symbolised all that was fine and stable and enduring in the Latin Empire, had fallen a prey to the ravage of barbarians. In such a world of instability and confusion, the Christian saw the Church as the one institution which, by virtue of its divine life, could survive the chaos of the time. Like a rock it would withstand the dissolution of the West. So it was that when Christians thought of the Church in that generation, they pictured to themselves not a community comprised of individual believers, but rather an institution ordained by God to be the means of eternal salvation.

The authority by which the Church spoke in its councils and by which the sacraments were administered by its clergy, he considered to be the authority of God. He made absolutely and exclusively the historic Catholic Church the medium of God's activity in the world. He denied to the Donatists and other heretics any participation in the gifts, graces, and sanctions that characterised the Church as the means of salvation. It is interesting to note that Augustine was the first to identify the existence of the Catholic Church with the millennium. In the early period Christian writers had generally reserved the term "Kingdom of God" for the future fulfilment of God's reign, that was to be ushered in by the return of Christ. But Augustine, in his exegesis of the passage in Revelation 20, contended that the millennium

[3]For a vivid account of what this event meant to the mind of the fifth century read Jerome's *Letter to Marcella* (Epistle 94).

was the period between the Incarnation and the Advent, and maintained that it was the visible reign of Christ in the Church on earth. His interpretation was directed against the Chiliasts, who anticipated in somewhat literal and crude terms an earthly kingdom of Christ in Jerusalem. It became of increasing importance in medieval theology, since it buttressed the claim of the Church to be the infallible rule of God in the world.

This was the static side of Augustine's thought. Although, as we have seen, his dynamic conception of the meaning of history prevented him from identifying the people in the visible Church with the elect of God, no such parallel idea can be seen in his doctrine of the Church as the channel of God's grace. He never for one moment hesitated to assert that the gospel, to which the historic Church witnessed, was the divine truth, and the sacraments that it administered were the very acts of God. It was this aspect of his teaching that had such profound influence through the course of medieval history, and was the basic presupposition on which the whole fabric of the medieval papacy was reared. It led to the development of the most extreme claims of the Church; and it was against this unwarranted identification of a particular institution with the sole channel of God's grace that the Reformers waged insistent and courageous warfare.

Yet we may readily sympathise with Augustine in his desire to avoid the error of the Donatists. In opposition to their idea that the grace of God was confined to a morally holy and perfect society, he pointed to the Church as the institution in history, wherein God's grace was made available as a free gift to the faithful who knew that they were far from perfect. But Augustine's solution of the problem led to other and grave difficulties. To identify a particular organisation with the sole instrument of God's grace in the world, seems quite as presumptuous as the

Donatist claim, and even more dangerous, since it avoids the
Donatist error. No historic Church can be the perfect medium
of God's activity for the very reason that Augustine himself advanced in considering the question of the Church and the elect.
No temporal manifestation of the Church can claim to be the
perfect embodiment of its eternal nature. Hence no particular
Church can speak with the absolute authority of God or claim
to be the sole medium of His grace. Any adequate idea of the
nature of the Church must do justice both to its temporal weakness and to its eternal glory. The divine quality in the Church
is that which transcends history, not that which is historical. The
visible Church is a human organisation; but insofar as it mediates
the life in Christ, insofar as it witnesses to the gospel of Christ
and ministers His sacraments, it speaks and acts with the authority
and by the power of God.

CHURCH AND STATE IN THE THOUGHT OF AUGUSTINE

The second grave problem that confronted the Church of
Augustine's day was its relation to the State. This was a question
which had previously been answered very simply. During the
years of persecution the Christians had been obedient to the laws
save where they conflicted with their religious convictions. It
was, however, when the rulers of the State became professing
Christians that the most difficult problems in the relation arose.
What were the limits of the imperial authority? Could the Christian faith be dictated to the nation? Should Emperors grant
privileges to the Catholic Church? Had the secular power the
right to stamp out heresy? Had it a right to tolerate or even to
favour heresy? What political activity was appropriate for the
clergy? These were practical issues of great significance and
most of them confront us in one form or another today.

Augustine saw that what was really involved in the whole issue was a philosophy of history. His great work, entitled *The Society of God,* was devoted to the construction of a Christian interpretation of history. The relation of the ecclesiastical to the secular power was only one phase of a greater problem, the meaning of Christian life in the world.

Augustine's work had a definite apologetic aim. It was written to defend the Church against pagan calumnies which attributed the sack of Rome by Alaric to the impiety of the Christians. To the heathen it seemed obvious that the overthrow of the old Roman devotions had been responsible for the anger of the gods, which was manifested in the barbarian invasions. *Pietas,* in the Roman mind, had a definite political as well as religious con-notation. It was believed that the fortunes of the Roman State were inseparably linked with the right traditional devotion to the Roman gods. In the first part of his work Augustine refuted this position, while in the second he attempted to give a Christian interpretation of these calamitous events. Turning the tables upon his accusers, he saw the sack of Rome as the judgment of God upon a wicked and impious civilisation.

Augustine's position is fundamentally religious and he views all human history as the struggle of two opposite and irrecon-cilable principles, faith and unbelief. Both are organised in vary-ing forms of human society, which in their temporal manifestations are the products of these two supra-historical realities, which he respectively calls the Society of God and the Society of the World. It would be wrong to imagine that Augustine identified com-pletely the earthly empires of the world with the god-defying spirit and the historic Catholic Church with the spirit of obedient faith. His language is admittedly at times misleading, but his meaning cannot be misunderstood. The identification is only partial in both cases. Just as the Catholic Church is the inadequate and temporal manifestation of that which it will ultimately become, so the Roman Empire cannot be conceived as wholly and intrinsically evil. Augustine often praises Rome for her virtue and her wars of justice, yet he sees every worldly society under the condemnation of God, for each in some measure incorporates and manifests the god-defying spirit.

Community or society, as it exists in the world, is nothing else than the expression of man's natural fellowship and has potentialities for good, no less than for evil. It is true that man's fallen nature precludes his establishing, by his own power, any true justice in human society; but that does not necessarily imply that all his social relationships are without an element of justice. That would be to deny the obvious facts of history. A kind of rough justice is the foundation of every state. This relative, natural, and incomplete harmony of men Augustine calls *concordia*, but he is well aware that every attempt to call this true justice is to blaspheme God and to evidence the god-defying spirit. The chief characteristic of this society of the world is to pose as God and to claim that what is human and relative has divine and eternal significance.

It is against this background that Augustine works out the relations of Church and State. The actual existence of earthly states, while arising out of this natural fellowship of men, he regards as a consequence of and a check upon sin. Every rough justice curbs the illicit passions of men. This was a Christian form of an idea originally Stoic and one which witnesses that Augustine never considered earthly states as the complete incarnation of evil. Thus between the Church and the State there exists a kind of harmony for the common preservation of the life of man; but the extent to which this harmony can be fully realised will depend upon the religious convictions of the secular authorities. The historic State which pretends to be God will naturally restrict this harmony, but the secular power which realises its own limitations will advance it, promoting the moral and religious welfare of the people.

The first function of the State is the preservation of external and internal peace. The defence of a country against unwarranted attack is the duty of every secular power and Augustine highly praises the universal peace under the Empire of Augustus. But to guard against internal dissension and strife is equally the concern of the State. Here the question of property is involved. Augustine holds that in the last resort it is in the hands of the State, which exercises a divinely appointed right over it to use it for the promotion of the common welfare. This is the argument he advances to defend the confiscation by the State of the property of heretics.

This leads to the second duty of the State. The secular power must promote the worship of the true God and exercise authority against idolatry and false worship. Being concerned with the true happiness of its people, the State cannot overlook the fact that this felicity is ultimately a religious question. Thus Augustine holds it is right for the Church to invoke the secular arm for the suppression of heresy. In his struggle with the Donatists he himself had had recourse to these measures, though it must be noted that the first appeal to the Emperor came from the heretics. In viewing Augustine's attitude on this question one must remember that the extreme Donatists had resorted to the wildest excesses of force and cruelty and their fanatical leaders had often endangered the peace and order of the State. Moreover, even in the face of this, Augustine admonished the proconsuls to adopt a course of wise and clement moderation.

But what if the State lends its support to any other religion than the true one? Augustine replies that the Christian then owes obedience to all laws save those that conflict with his obligation to worship God. Here he reserves the right of conscience to obey God rather than man.

In the ideal State, however, the situation is entirely different. The relations of Church and State are those of mutual dependence and reciprocal obligation. This was the conception which dominated the medieval civilisation and although the ecclesiastical and political officials were engaged in a long and bitter struggle for the final supremacy, the underlying idea of the relationship was derived from Augustine.

In conclusion, we may note the strength and weakness of Augustine's position. When he considers history from the dynamic point of view of the warfare of the society of God with the society of the world, his insight is profound. The god-defying spirit of earthly states is something which modern political experiments have again exemplified, and with Augustine we are well aware of the conflict of the two societies. On the other hand, when he thinks of the Catholic Church in the static terms of the true Church, which the State must uphold against heresy, we see the weakness of his position. He tends to regard the historic Catholic organisation as the sole institution to which has been committed the truth of religion and worship. The danger that faces Augustine's position is that the Catholic organisation may become a god-defying Church, which sets itself up as God upon earth.

AMBROSE AND CHRYSOSTOM

Behind Augustine's theory of the relations of Church and State lies an historical situation in the West, which contrasts vividly with the political fortunes of the Church in the East. By the early fifth century the Western Church had gained political power. The removal of the seat of imperial authority to Constantinople had left the Church in the West free to develop its jurisdiction without too great proximity to the highest political authority. Indeed, the Roman popes in many ways became the heirs of the Cæsars and transformed the former political sovereignty of Rome into an ecclesiastical power. This was equally true of the episcopal dignity in other great cities. Among these Milan held a prominent place. It was strategically situated on the trade routes of the Empire and was a military and imperial centre of great importance. The Bishop of Milan became an official whose authority was not limited to purely ecclesiastical functions. He often undertook political missions of grave consequence and no sharp division was drawn between the ecclesiastical and secular authority.

In the East, on the other hand, the Church came almost completely under the domination of the Emperor. The Bishop of Constantinople was regarded as an imperial official and the pre-eminence of his see was due entirely to the political eminence of New Rome. Constantinople could boast neither apostolical foundation nor the blood of martyrs, and was dependent upon the imperial power for its superior dignity. The contrast between the Bishop of old Rome and the Bishop of Constantinople was most marked in this regard. The former was the successor of Saint Peter, the Prince of Apostles: the latter was the first ecclesiastical official of the Byzantine Empire. The Eastern Church tended to become a national Church, controlled by the Emperor. The ideal relationship between the royal and priestly authorities was regarded as an organic union. The State was to defend and guide the Church, by whose spiritual power it would be gradually transformed. Nevertheless, the close contact with the secular government easily reduced the position of the Church to one of a state department of religion. The Western Church, on the other hand, boasted and exerted an independence of all secular authority. It claimed a superior power by divine right, to which even Emperors must bow, and the disintegrating political situation in the West prevented its being hampered by the close control of the secular government.

The fortunes of two fourth-century bishops, Ambrose of Milan and Chrysostom of Constantinople, well reflect this contrast between the East and the West. Ambrose won successive triumphs against the imperial power and even forced an emperor to do public penance. Chrysostom died in exile, having dared to raise his voice in criticism of the Empress and the Court.

Born of noble parentage, the young Ambrose was trained to enter the legal profession and having gained high repute in his calling received the civil appointment of consular magistrate, with his court at Milan. On the death of the bishop of that city, Ambrose came down to Milan to keep the peace, foreseeing the vehement strife that generally characterised episcopal elections. During his speech in the church, where he was advocating to the people peaceful measures for arriving at the decision some one in the congregation shouted out, "Ambrose for Bishop!" The popularity of the young official was such that the cry met with general approbation. Despite his unwillingness to accept, Ambrose found the episcopate virtually forced upon him. Though an earnest Christian he was as yet unbaptised,[4] and he passed through the various orders of the Church with unprecedented rapidity. Within eight days he was consecrated bishop.

[4]It was a common custom in the Early Church to delay baptism. People shrunk with a certain religious awe from this momentous event and this was enhanced by the gravity with which sin after baptism was regarded.

Once in the office he devoted himself to his duties with zeal and courage. His money and lands he gave to the poor. He preached with fervour and regularity, his style graced by its directness and earnestness rather than its flowering oratory. This was a trait characteristically Western and contrasted with the imagery and flowery utterance of the Greek pulpit. Augustine attributed his conversion to this godly bishop. Ambrose schooled himself in the strictest ascetic practices and not a little of his religious devotion was marked by the tendency to interpret Christianity in realistic and sometimes rather material terms. For instance, he highly praised his brother for tying a napkin containing some of the Eucharistic elements around his neck for safety when he was shipwrecked.

It is, however, his political influence which must here concern us. His first triumph was the success that greeted his appeal to the imperial power which had almost been prevailed upon by the Prefect of Rome to restore the pagan altar of Victory in the Senate. He was entrusted by Justina, the mother of the young Emperor, Valentinian the Second, with the delicate mission to the usurper Maximus in Gaul. But it was with Justina that his first bitter quarrel with the secular authority was fought. She espoused the cause of the heretic Arians and demanded one of the Milan churches for their services. Ambrose, considering himself the guardian of the orthodoxy of Milan, refused to allow such desecration of a church building. He further refused the proposal to concede the large basilica for their partial use. Justina replied by sending soldiers to hang the purple curtains on another Milan church (the Portian basilica), thus claiming it for the imperial treasury. Ambrose heard of it while he was celebrating the Eucharist in the large basilica. He sent some of his clergy to try and prevent bloodshed which this act was likely to cause, as the people were on his side. Ambrose himself finally went to the church and occupied it for several days, keeping up the spirits of the people by the singing of hymns, which he introduced in imitation of the Eastern custom. The political officials demanded that he concede to the Emperor his rights: Ambrose replied that the Emperor had no rights over the Church of God. The struggle finally terminated in the triumph of Ambrose and the reply he sent to the court chamberlain well illustrates his determined and courageous stand. This official had said, "Whilst I am alive shall you despise Valentinian? I will cut off your head first." To which Ambrose answered, "May God grant you to fulfil what you threaten; for then my fate will be that of a bishop, your act will be that of a eunuch."

The conflict of Ambrose with Theodosius is even more famous. It seems that the officer and garrison in Thessalonica had been slain by the mob. The city had for some time been discontent with the quartering of barbarian troops that had been forced on them. The actual outrage was provoked by the commandant's imprisoning a popular charioteer and refusing to release him for the circus games. The brutal action of the populace aroused the fiery anger and resentment of the Emperor Theodosius, and he replied by a wholesale massacre of some 7000 of the inhabitants. The conscience of Christians everywhere was instantly outraged; and when the news reached Ambrose, he wrote a determined and courageous letter to Theodosius, demanding that he manifest his public repentance of so vehement and ill-judged an action, and warning him that he could not admit him to the Eucharist while his hands were so stained with blood. The letter provoked from the historian, Gibbon, the remark that it was "a miserable rhapsody on a noble subject," but the criticism is manifestly unjust. The high moral courage of Ambrose may

well arouse our admiration. He denounces the Emperor's deed
not without a sense of his own humility and not unmindful of
the sincere Christian conviction that Theodosius had often dis-
played. It is not a blast against the Emperor, it is a measured
and wise appeal that he publicly repent for this outburst of
vehemence and unrestrained temper. The precise outcome of
Ambrose's letter is not clear. The historical records of the penance
of the Emperor conflict in detail. Yet behind them there is certainly a basis of truth that Theodosius bowed to the judgment
of Ambrose and, stripping himself of his royal insignia, made
public penance for his crime.

No incident in this period so captivates the imagination and
demonstrates the power of the Church. Ambrose lived up to
his belief that there was nothing more dangerous or base than
for a priest to fail to utter his convictions freely. The dauntless
courage of the Church in such circumstances gave a practical
as well as a theoretical significance to the tenet that ecclesiastical
authority was superior to secular. Ambrose's dictum that priests
should be the judges of the laity, not the laity of the priests,
became the claim of the medieval Church; and this incident gave
a precedent for its superior power. The danger, however, inherent
in the exercise of such an authority is that it should be dictated
by purely selfish aims and accompanied with less judicious
moderation and with more overweening pride. This was the
besetting sin of the medieval papacy which identified the Roman
Catholic Church with the Church of God, and often used its
power to further ecclesiastical policies which were far from
righteous or spiritual.

From the triumphs of Ambrose we turn to the tragic fate of
John Chrysostom—John "of the golden mouth," as he was nicknamed, for the splendour of his oratory. He, too, was not lacking

in moral courage or Christian devotion, but his efforts to reform
the court failed to advance the power of the Church and brought
him a lonely exile.

Like Ambrose he was trained for the law and for a while
practised as an advocate with a brilliant career ahead of him.
However, under the influence of Basil, his friend and the com-
panion of his studies, he left his profession for the pursuit of
the "true philosophy," by which he meant the ascetic life. He
transformed his home into a miniature monastery and led a life
of the severest discipline. His long emaciated limbs led him to
compare himself to a spider and the rigour of his ascetic life
left an ineradicable mark upon his character. His gloomy, aloof,
and somewhat contumacious disposition was often the cause of
friction with his enemies and hid the more delightful and amiable
side of his nature.

Ordained to the priesthood in Antioch, he preached to wildly
enthusiastic congregations. His sermons are masterpieces of the
vivid, picturesque, and poetic oratory of Eastern preaching. He
frequently had to bid the congregation to refrain from applauding,
and so popular was his preaching among the wealthy that he had
to warn them of lurking pickpockets who found these rich Christians, so easily carried away by the power of his oratory, a source
of easy gain.

Called to the episcopate of Constantinople, he entered a city
of lively and troublous factions. His predecessor had been definitely
worldly and had enjoyed the pomp and ceremony of a rich
church. John's ascetic nature revolted from such ostentation. He
raised money by selling the costly plate of the church to aid
hospitals and tried to reform the morals of the clergy. Such dis-
ciplinary measures met with stern opposition but, when he dared
even to attack the lax manners of the court, his downfall became

inevitable. Yet by the vigour of his moral courage and the force of his eloquence he had gathered a large following and grew increasingly powerful. This, together with his denunciations of the court and his mockery of the rich attire of noble women, aroused the jealousy of the Empress Eudoxia, who proved his fatal enemy. Chrysostom was the only man in the way of her complete control of the East, for she had long since learned how to manage her husband, Arcadius. She gathered around her a small body of friends who were determined on Chrysostom's downfall. As the opposition increased Chrysostom grew more reckless. In a sermon he hinted at a comparison of the Empress with Jezebel and thus laid himself open to severe charges. The patriarch of Alexandria, always jealous of the power of the new see of Constantinople, came forward as the leader of Eudoxia's cabal against Chrysostom, and, on a trumped-up charge that he was harbouring heretics, had him condemned at the Synod of Oak. He was accused of the most contemptible charges which included gluttony and inciting to rebellion. His banishment aroused popular fervour and the city was in an uproar. A timely earthquake drove Eudoxia into a panic about her soul, and frightened in conscience she manipulated the return of the bishop and the revocation of the council's decrees.

Chrysostom remained adamant in opposition to her. Reconciliation was only temporary and again he indulged in attacks on the Empress in his sermons. She had erected a column of porphyry and a silver statue to herself and rites that were almost heathen were held in her honour during the Church services. Chrysostom thundered in his preaching, "Herodias is dancing again!" His enemies were now determined on a final banishment and a new decree to this effect was passed at the Council of Antioch. But to get rid of Chrysostom was not so easy. The

Emperor feared mob riots and violence and hesitated to put the decree into effect. The situation, however, was brought to a climax by a tragic incident on the Vigil of the Resurrection. Three thousand catechumens had assembled for baptism in the Church of Saint Sophia. Chrysostom was there, although he had been forbidden to administer the sacraments. The stillness of the night was broken by the clash of arms and wild barbarian soldiers, at the command of the Emperor, broke into the church to seize the bishop. The catechumens reassembled in the baths of Constantine, but were followed by the Thracian soldiers, who perpetrated every violence and outrage. Palladius, an eyewitness, remarks, "The waters of regeneration were stained with blood." Two unsuccessful attempts were made on Chrysostom's life and finally he was forced into banishment by Arcadius. As he left, the Church of Saint Sophia burst into flames, and though efforts were made to trace the fire, by torture and other means, they were unavailing.

Chrysostom in exile presents a tragic but a noble figure. During the trying and perilous journey to the scene of his banishment, a mountain village in Armenia, his health broke down completely and he was sick with fever. He only lived three years longer, but the letters he wrote from his exile reveal the wide influence that he exerted from this place of desolation. He was consulted by a multitude of churches on every conceivable problem and the range of his administration in this little mountain village is almost incredible. The historian Suidas says, "Only the omnipotent God can recount his writings," and, although most of these were written before his exile, the statement bears witness to his tireless energy.

After his death the new Emperor, Theodosius II, had his body brought back to Constantinople, and tried to make atonement for the wrongs inflicted on him. But this could never undo the tragic circumstances of the Byzantine Church, to which the fate of Chrysostom witnesses. Its subjection to the imperial power continued a characteristic of the Byzantine Empire. It is true that the organic fusion of Church and State in the East did not leave the Church without a measure of power, and none of the Emperors who attempted to support heresy (from Constantius to Leo the Isaurian) were finally triumphant. Nevertheless, the fortunes of the Byzantine Church contrast vividly with those of the Church in the West.

Chapter IV

THE CHURCH IN THE LIFE AND THOUGHT OF THE MIDDLE AGES

INTRODUCTION

To UNDERSTAND the Church in the Middle Ages it must be realised that the unity of the medieval world was ecclesiastical rather than political. Out of the chaos of the barbarian invasions and the downfall of the Latin Empire emerged a Christian civilisation with the Catholic Church as its centre and foundation. The Church gave meaning and direction to medieval life. It claimed and exerted an authority superior to that of all territorial princes: it was the conserver of learning and culture during the dark days of ravage by successive invasions: it inherited the power and dignity of the old imperial régime. Popes became the successors of the Cæsars and the ancient cohesion of the Latin Empire was transformed into the unity of Catholic Europe. The Church with its extensive organisation, with its political, economic, and spiritual power, claimed to be the sole and ultimate authority in the world. It demanded the obedience of secular princes no less than of the meanest serf. It interpreted the will of God in every relationship of life, from the course of international diplomacy to the daily conduct of the poorest Christian. It stood as the representative of God in the world: the Divine authority to which had been committed the keys of heaven and hell. While the decisions of the Church did not pass altogether unchallenged, and while it was often forced to compromise with political authorities and local tradition, nevertheless, the general course of medieval history is only intelligible in the light of the fact that men believed these supernatural claims of the Church. The medieval man did not doubt that the Church's excommunication really deprived his soul of salvation and he was equally convinced that its indulgences relieved him of temporal punishment in Purgatory. It is impossible for Protestants even vaguely to conceive what this meant to the medieval mind, and the most sympathetic imagination is awed no less than repelled by the extravagance of these claims of the Church and by their well-nigh universal acceptance. The historical circumstances that attended this rise of the Roman Catholic Church can be examined, but its inner meaning constantly eludes us. In that age the Church gave tangible and exact expression to God's demands on men. It confronted them with revelation and consoled them with redemption. In the Mass, which was the centre of the religious life of the Middle Ages, the grace of God was mediated to man and the sacrifice of Christ on Calvary was re-enacted in a drama of momentous significance. By the supernatural power of his office, the priest changed the inner reality of a wafer into God Himself, and so made it possible for the believer to partake of the Divine nature for his redemption.

The Church was the Will of God on earth. It represented that static tradition of the institution, which we have already studied in Augustine. To the Reformers it appeared the greatest blasphemy in history: to the men of the Middle Ages it was the highest consolation and assurance: to the historian it will long remain the profoundest attempt to build a Christian civilisation. By identifying itself with the interests of its age and culture and by partially transcending them, it was, at its height and at its best, the most ambitious and in many ways the most mature embodiment of the Christian Faith. Its tragedy lies in the contrast between the arrogance of its claims and the magnificence of its achievement.

CHURCH AND STATE

We have already pointed out the great difference in the development of Christian East and West. In the former, the close proximity of the Church to the Byzantine State forbade its pursuing an independent course. In the West, on the other hand, the way was open for the Church to play a more original and creative rôle. It had to triumph over the forces of chaos and disorder, while in the East the Church had to compromise with a firmly rooted cultural tradition. Furthermore, the Latin Church fell heir to the ancient seat of Imperial authority, which the removal of the Emperors to Constantinople had left open for a successor. The Latin genius for law and order and its practical sense of social responsibility were given a Christian meaning and direction. Imperial Rome became Christian Rome and the Popes became the spiritual Cæsars of Western Christendom.

They summed up in themselves a variety of ancient offices of the old Empire, giving each a new and Christian interpretation. The austere and simple sermons of Pope Leo I reveal him in the office of censor, caring for the morals of his people. As prætor the Pope declared and defined the law of the Church. Since the fourth century, churches in many parts of Europe had been known to appeal to Rome as the final arbiter and judge of ecclesiastical cases, and the shrewd and careful wisdom of the papal decisions, both in theological and practical issues, aided not a little this increasing power. Finally, as Cæsar, the Pope extended an imperial jurisdiction over the Latin world, a jurisdiction based not on a civil authority but on the authority of the apostolical tradition of which he was both guardian and interpreter.

The Christian Church, fresh and vigorous after its long conflict with its persecutors, represented in the West a vitality and youth that contrasted strangely with the senile despair and decay into which the old Empire had fallen with the barbarian invasions. Well aware of the impotence and incompetence of the Eastern Empire to save Europe during these tragic years, men turned to the Church as the one sure foundation and hope in the midst of chaos. It was not to Ravenna, the seat of the Exarch, the Western representative of the Byzantine Empire, but to Rome, the city of the Popes, that the eyes of men were diverted.

The Latin Church was not slow to take advantage of this situation and a succession of three able Popes laid the foundations of the papal power. When Pope Innocent I returned to Rome after the ravage by Alaric he found his authority unlimited. The barbarian had destroyed the last vestiges of the ancient pagan city and made possible the building of Christian Rome. Leo I himself went out at the head of an embassy to meet Attila, the invading Hun, and so overcome was the barbarian warrior with the grave and religious dignity of so great a man that he consented to retire from Italy. No less successful was Gregory the Great, who a century later made peace with the Lombards and is supposed to have met the invader, Agilulph, on the steps of Saint Peter's. Once again a Pope so awed the invading barbarian that he broke up the siege of the city. Though the legend is doubtless exaggerated it does justice to the initiative and authority of Gregory.

The papal sovereignty, however, was built on foundations more sure than these. Its territorial independence was assured by its acquisition of lands from the gifts of the faithful. Among these estates were many of the rich wheat fields of Sicily. After the Vandal conquests of North Africa and the diversion of the Egyptian grain ships to Constantinople (following the removal of the imperial seat to the East), these became the main source of supply for the city of Rome. Thus the papacy was not without an important economic power. The extension of its authority was further guaranteed by its missionary activity. In the monks, who undertook these missions, the Popes found spiritual armies who converted the heathen and the heretic not only to Christianity but to the Roman Church. The monasteries in the furthest parts of Europe became centres of the papal authority. It was not without reason that the destruction of the monasteries was undertaken by the Reformed countries centuries later. They were important strongholds of the papal power, and they vitally contributed to the recovery of the papacy after it had sunk to its lowest ebb in the tenth century.

To the Patrimony of Peter and to the missionary success of the Church there was added a political alliance with the new rising power of Europe, the Kingdom of the Franks. By extending a religious sanction to the Carolingian dynasty and allowing the last of the feeble Merovingian kings to be deposed and shut up in a monastery, the Church bound to itself a powerful political ally. Pepin the Short (the new Frankish king) assisted the Church against the increasing menace of the Lombards in Italy and advanced its territorial acquisitions by lavish gifts. From this day date the States of the Church, the complete and independent rule over which the Latin Church maintained till the nineteenth century. These States guaranteed the Church from close political domination and prevented the Bishop of Rome from becoming merely the first bishop of Italy. That is why the main factor in papal diplomacy during the succeeding centuries was to hinder every attempt at the unification of Italy. Only when he was territorially independent could the Pope exert his influence over the course of European affairs and be free from local political ties and obligations. Hence, the recovery as an independent possession of a small part of his former lands was of such importance to the Pope in the recent Concordat with Mussolini. The Pope claims to be the spiritual head of Christendom not only the first bishop of national Italy, although it must be admitted that the pressure of the modern Italian state has severely limited his freedom.

In large measure the claims advanced by the Church were a restatement and development of that side of Augustine's thought which identified the visible Catholic Church with the will of God upon earth. The Church was the sole channel of salvation in the world. It spoke with the authority of God and there was no power or jurisdiction superior to it on earth.

In one important particular the development of the papal theory was an advance upon Augustine's position. The African Father does not refer frequently in his writings to the papacy, though when he does he accords it a certain honour and pre-eminence which is not exactly defined. It is interesting that he retracted his first interpretation of Matthew 16:18, where he had contended that the Church had been built on Peter and his successors in the Roman See. His later exegesis of the passage referred the foundation of the Church to Peter's confession of Christ as Messiah rather than to Peter himself, and in another place Augustine stressed the fact that the keys of heaven and hell were given not to Peter individually but to the whole Church represented by him. The independent attitude of the Church of North Africa confirms this position. In the case of Apiarius the Council of

Carthage had written that "the assumption of the appeal to Rome is a trespass upon the rights of the African Church."

Since the days of Augustine, however, the papal power had gradually increased and this practical jurisdiction of Rome was matched by highly developed claims. While they date back a century earlier, they reach their clearest expression in Leo I. The Pope is regarded as the successor of Saint Peter, the Prince of Apostles, to whom was committed the final authority of the whole Church. The Bishop of Rome is the door-keeper of heaven, the shepherd of the Universal Church and the guardian of the apostolical tradition. On him devolves, from Peter, the fullness of all power (*plenitudo potestatis*), and he is without equal or superior in the world. From him flows all authority and every gift and grace that the Church enjoys. To separate oneself from the Roman Church is to cut oneself off from the divine blessings which are mediated only through the papacy. Again and again through the Middle Ages these claims were asserted and exercised. A famous eleventh-century document, the *Dictatus Papae,* states that the "Church has never erred and will never err to all eternity." The final definition of papal infallibility in 1870 was but a logical consequence of a doctrine which had been at the root of the papal power from these early days.

While the ecclesiastical absoluteness of the Roman See was definitely established by the fifth century, the relation of this divine authority to the secular power was not yet clearly defined. The coronation of Charlemagne by Leo III on Christmas Day 800 A.D. marks a turning point in European history and in many ways this is a symbolic date. It can be regarded as the foundation of the Holy Roman Empire, the secular counterpart of the Holy Catholic Church. Viewed as a unity working in harmony, the Empire and the Church promised to be the beginning of the

Kingdom of God on earth. The ideal state of Augustine, promoting the worship of the true God and recognising the Church as the visible expression of God's spiritual authority in the world had been realised.

In this event there was implied a grave problem. Which of the two authorities was superior? To Augustine the relationship had been one of mutual obligation and reciprocal responsibility. In history, however, such a relationship is impossible to achieve. The rights of the two powers had more clearly to be defined, and in that definition there was involved the lust for power on the part of the papacy no less than on the part of the Empire.

The fact that Leo had crowned Charlemagne was itself a precedent that could be taken to demonstrate the superior power of the papacy. But its meaning lies deeper than this. The event marks the commencement of that long struggle of the Church with the State, which dominated the course of medieval history. We have already seen that the alliance of the Church with Pepin proved of great advantage for the papacy. This was due to the fact that between Rome and the political power of the Franks stood the Lombard kingdom in North Italy. The Pope's independence and his freedom from secular control were thus guaranteed. When, however, Charlemagne extended the bounds of the Frankish kingdom far beyond the wildest dreams of Pepin, and constructed an empire that reached from the Pyrenees to beyond the east banks of the Elbe and included Northern Italy, the papacy no longer remained free from secular interference. The Pope tended to become the first bishop of the Empire rather than universal bishop of Christendom. He was constantly in danger of having his authority limited by the force of secular arms. What is more, Charlemagne atempted to align the interests of the Church with those of the Empire by the restoration of the metropolitans. The unification of the Church under the highly centralised system of archbishops and provincial synods was carried through to the detriment of ecclesiastical independence; for it was the Emperor rather than the Pope who stood at its apex.

Charlemagne wanted an Empire of which he alone was the head and in which the Church functioned as a department of the State. The struggle was thus initiated between two conceptions of the nature and function of the Christian Church. On the one hand, the papacy claimed to be the final authority in the world, independent of every secular power: indeed, it was later urged that princes received their authority through the papacy and not directly from God. On the other hand, the princes, and in particular the Emperor, claimed to hold their secular authority independently of the Church and deemed that the papal power only extended to matters spiritual. To understand this it must be remembered that the medieval mind approached everything from the religious point of view. It was conceived with Christian insight that all power derived from above and not from below: that kings and popes alike were the subjects of God and owed their allegiance to Him.

The conflict was between the Catholic Church as the supreme authority in the world, the ultimate source and meaning of all spiritual and earthly power, and the territorial Church as a limited authority, allied with local and secular interests. While the Emperors never denied the spiritual jurisdiction of the papacy they tended to limit its exercise by claiming for themselves an independent secular power, extending to the material aspects of the Church's life. Ecclesiastical lands and wealth, which through the Middle Ages grew to immense proportions, were to be subject to the secular authority and thus the interests of the Church would be inseparably united with those of the local territory.

To appreciate this we must examine briefly the nature of feudalism, the social system that underlay the medieval development. The basic need that feudalism attempted to meet was one of territorial security during the declining years of the old Empire and the havoc and chaos of the barbarian invasions. It was a social system resting on three foundations. There was first the Teutonic custom of tenure of land in return for military service. This provided security both for the tenant and for the landowner. Then there was the Latin conception of law. All relationships were conceived as permanent legal contracts. This law was not something imposed from without, but was rooted in the very nature of social relationships and as such was inviolable and sacred. Finally, there was the Christian faith, which gave meaning and direction to the system, asserting that the primary factor in these relationships was religious. The obedience of the ruled could not be understood apart from the obligation of the ruler. Both were the children of God and to both were allotted their appropriate spheres. The dependence of one man upon another was not an occasion of exploiting another's needs. Rather was it a sacred relationship in which power involved duty. The lord owed his dependant security, no less than the dependant owed his lord obedience. Neither side of the contract could be broken without violating the law of God, the supreme Overlord of all.

This idea was basic to the structure of medieval society where the highest good was looked upon as order. Christendom, a concept which has now lost its deepest meaning, was a living ideal for the Middle Ages. Men viewed society as an organic whole, united by a common faith, ruled by divinely appointed authorities and distributed into fixed classes according to their function and vocation. Each man owed society duties and claimed from society privileges according to his rank. All were members one of another, each had his station, each his rights and obligations which were grounded in the law of God. Although this ideal was never completely realised, it exerted the most powerful influence on the medieval mind.

Territorial security was of vital moment during the years of invasion, which continued with the intrusion of the Scandinavian Norsemen until the eleventh century. To the secular ruler, it was important to provide a centralised government, which guaranteed security to all parts of his domain. That was the premature attempt of Charlemagne, although his kingdom collapsed after his death, since it was founded more upon himself than upon an enduring system. However, the same idea was to be revived with greater and more lasting success a century and a half later with the rise to power of the German Emperors. The part to be played by the Church in this imperial scheme was plainly one of identifying its interests with those of the local authorities and yielding its material power to the central secular government. The ecclesiastical system which incorporated this idea was known as lay patronage and lay investiture. The local noble had the appointment of the clergy and invested them with the insignia of their office. He was sure to elect men who would do his bidding and, when necessary, further his purposes by providing means and soldiers to protect his land. He sought to control the extensive landed possessions of the Church.

This is precisely what the ecclesiastics refused to accord him. From the religious point of view such a system endangered the authority of the Church, bringing it under secular sway. The papacy maintained that the Church's wealth and all the persons, lay as well as ecclesiastic, holding its lands or dependent upon it, constituted a kingdom free from secular control. It demanded a system of jurisdiction entirely separate from that of the courts of the land. One of the most effective measures by which the Church was able to assert its claims was by insisting upon the celibacy of the clergy. A man who has neither wife nor children is not concerned in the local interests of his community and has no other obligation than that to the Church. He is not immersed in the practical affairs of life or entangled in securing the welfare of a family. Although the celibacy of the clergy sometimes brought with it gross immorality and was far from being strictly observed, it did provide the Church with a powerful weapon in its warfare with the State.

The Church was not content merely to declare the immunity of its decrees and possessions from secular control. It went a step further and tried to become the State. It claimed that since the feudal system was rooted in a religious obligation which was sealed by an oath of fidelity, it was in the power of the popes to release subjects from their oath, when wicked rulers had transgressed their side of the contract. Popes could thus depose emperors and set up their own secular rulers who would be amenable to the Church's interests. The lust for power thus had as ample opportunity to corrupt the Church as it had to corrupt the State. The great popes claimed, in the famous words of Boniface VIII, that the imperial sword[1] was to be wielded "at the consent and permission of the priest," and though this definition came at the beginning of the fourteenth century, it aptly summarises the contention of the Church as early as the eleventh.

---

[1] The Church interpreted the two swords, referred to in Luke 22:38, as the spiritual and temporal authority in the world. One of the earliest attempts of the Church to claim ultimate temporal as well as spiritual authority in the West is found in the *Donation of Constantine,* a forged document of the ninth century purporting to be a letter of Constantine to Pope Sylvester. In it the Emperor after demanding that all ecclesiastics should be subject to the Roman See goes on to announce his decision to donate the lands of the western world to the Pope and his successors. Thus on the removal of the seat of imperial authority to the East, the Pope will be supreme ruler of the West.

By the favour of the popes princes ruled and to the papal jurisdiction they were to be subject in all matters. Thus, if on the
one hand the limitations of the Church's rights by the secular
power tended to swallow up the Church in the State, on the other
hand the papal claims tended in the opposite direction and would
have swallowed up the State in the Church.

CANOSSA

An incident taken from the eleventh century will serve to illustrate the hard-fought battle of Pope against Emperor. The struggle
of Hildebrand with Henry IV gives an indication of the great
power of the papacy, a power which seems wildly romantic and
almost incredible to the modern mind. Yet it instances at the
same time the weakness of the papal authority, for in some ways
the final victory was with the imperial power. While the picture
of an Emperor standing in penitence in the snows outside Canossa
may indicate the temporary triumph of the Church, yet the force
of arms was often more significant than the spiritual power of
the Pope in determining the course of history.

The two contestants in this struggle make a strange contrast.
Hildebrand was a man whose origin was as obscure and humble
as his bearing was unimposing. He was of small stature, un-
gainly, and with a feeble voice. His enemies nicknamed him by
the diminutive "Hildebrandellus." Yet his fiery and restless eyes
reflected something of his vigorous character. Of his early life we
know little. He may have become a monk, and was certainly connected at one time with the monastery of St. Paul, in Rome. He
came into close contact with the Cluniac Movement, though the
tradition that he was ever the prior of the convent is in error.
The importance of this monastic reform cannot be overemphasised.
From Cluny came the champions of the ideal of the Church, pure

and regenerate, free from secular control and independent in its own right. They insisted rigidly upon the celibacy of the clergy, resisted every attempt to corrupt the Church by simony and lay investiture, and instituted a thorough reform of the lax practices and morals of the clergy.

Hildebrand was an ecclesiastical statesman of foresight and wisdom, possessed of indomitable will and courage. He was the mind behind the papal throne during five successive administrations, and knew well how to control the situation without holding the leading office. He ruled through others, until finally he was called to the papal chair in 1073, taking the name Gregory VII. When his struggle with the imperial power reached its height, Hildebrand was a man of middle age with years of mature experience behind him. His aims were clearly formulated and definite: his character was incorruptible.

On the opposite side was the Emperor, Henry IV, who was graced neither with the mature wisdom nor with the unswerving resolution of his opponent. He was still in his twenties when the conflict with Hildebrand came to a head. He was a man of passionate nature and of somewhat unstable character. He inherited the ambition of the German Emperors since Otto I, to create a centralised political authority which would crush the power of the feudal nobles and extend its power south of the Alps to Italy.[2] His father, Henry III, had attempted to carry out this purpose by vesting the imperial office with a religious dignity and devoting himself seriously to the reform of the Church, which, since the fall of the Carolingian Empire, had sunk into the period of its worst decay and decline. He rescued the papacy from a de-

[2]The ill-fated attempt of the German Emperors to create such an Empire, which was the traditional territorial division since the treaty of Verdun (843), was doomed to failure because of its geographical impossibility. Whenever they moved south to Italy the opportunity was given in Germany for the revolt of the feudal nobles.

plorable schism in which the papal tiara had been bartered for money and was responsible for the election of the strong reforming Pope, Leo IX. But he bequeathed to his son two grave problems which arose out of this attempt to create a centralised German authority closely allied with the papacy.[3] The feudal nobles in Saxony and South Germany resisted the imperial encroachments on their former feudal power, while the papacy, once set on the road to reform, was sternly opposed to any imperial interference. Though the Church had been rescued from its decline by the domineering policy of Henry III, Leo IX and his successors claimed complete freedom from all secular control. Thus the policies of Pope and Emperor came into clear and open conflict. The former demanded complete independence of all territorial interests and restrictions. The latter envisaged a united and centralised Empire, in which the imperial and papal interests would be essentially one. To achieve such an alliance the secular control of all ecclesiastical appointments was essential. The imperial power could brook no rival.

The issue came to a head over the episcopal elections in Milan, a city which held a key position in the military, control of northern Italy. Its archbishop was an ecclesiastical and political official of no small importance. It seems that Henry IV had taken upon himself to fill the See directly it fell vacant, appointing a man, Godfrey of Castiglione, and securing his consecration to the office. A rival candidate, Atto, was chosen by the "Pataria," the "Ragbags" or popular party in Milan, which sided with the papacy against the imperial control of the city. The Pope, Alexander II, recognised Atto as the true archbishop and excom-

[3]Both from the economic and military points of view the alliance with the ecclesiastical nobles was of vital moment to the Emperor. The fact, moreover, that their offices and the wealth and power they entailed were not hereditary, made the possibility of the imperial control far greater than in the case of the secular nobility.

municated Godfrey. Alexander died a few days later, bequeathing the struggle to his successor, Hildebrand.

The new Pope held two synods in 1075, condemning the action of Henry, forbidding all lay investiture, and even excommunicating five of the Emperor's councillors for simony (*i.e.*, traffic in ecclesiastical offices). He wrote to the Emperor, calling him to account and threatening him with excommunication unless he yielded to the papal wishes. Henry, who had met with success against the revolting Saxon nobles and was temporarily master of Germany, replied by holding a council in Worms. Surrounded by his own ecclesiastical followers, he deposed Hildebrand from office. He claimed he was nothing but a "false monk," and concluded his letter with the words, "Come down, come down and be damned through all eternity."

The counter-reply of Hildebrand is one of the most famous documents of the Middle Ages. As the successor of Peter, Prince of Apostles, and in the name of Almighty God, he excommunicated Henry, deposing him from "the Kingdom of the Teutons and of Italy," and releasing all Christians from their oath of obligation to him. The medieval world was profoundly shocked by this deposition of the Emperor, and while the claims of the Church may have been precarious even in those days, the political circumstances of the moment were more favourable for Hildebrand than for Henry. The Saxons renewed their revolt and the secular nobles sided with the papacy, ever fearing that the creation of a strong centralised government would limit the exercise of their local authority. At the Diet of Tribur (October, 1076) on the Rhine, the disaffected nobles demanded that Henry negotiate with the Pope and get himself released from the excommunication. If he failed to do this within a year they threatened to withdraw their allegiance from him and create a new Emperor. They also invited the Pope to a council in Augsburg in 1077, which would consider the whole political and religious situation in Germany. On the other bank of the river at Oppenheim, Henry took up his position, but after fruitless negotiations he was forced by his subjects into submission to the papacy. He promised to yield "fitting reverence and obedience to the apostolic office," and pledged that he would either give evidence of the crimes imputed to him or else undergo the penance demanded by the Pope. He waited several gloomy months in the city of Speyer, cut off from the Church and from the exercise of his imperial power. Finally, he decided there was only one thing to do. He must prevent the Pope's coming to Augsburg, which he saw as his imminent ruin. Therefore, in the depth of winter—one of the severest recorded in history—and attended only by his wife and infant son and a few retainers, he made the long and perilous journey across the Alps.

The Pope was residing in the castle of Canossa, in Lombardy, waiting to pursue his journey to Augsburg. Henry remained outside the castle, "barefoot and clad only in wretched woollen garments, beseeching us with tears to grant him absolution and forgiveness" (as the letter of the Pope to the German princes describes the incident). For three days (January 25-28, 1077) he waited thus in the snows of Canossa, a royal suppliant before the Pope. Finally, when Hildebrand thought that Henry's humiliation was complete, and that he was truly repentant, he opened the door to him and "removed the excommunication from him and received him again into the bosom of the Holy Mother Church." Henry then took an oath promising to satisfy the grievances against him in accordance with the conditions of the papacy.

Who had really won? Temporarily the imperial dignity had been forced to bow to the Church and had been involved in the deepest humiliation. The dramatic act at Canossa has become symbolic of the high-water mark of the papal power. Yet this victory was but shortlived. Henry had accomplished his purpose and forestalled the action at Augsburg. Two months later civil war broke out in Germany and the enemies of Henry, some of them outraged by the imperial degradation, most of them seizing the opportunity to advance their private interests, set up a rival Emperor, Rudolph. The Pope vacillated awhile in his choice of sides, but finally (in 1080) he decided against Henry, fulminating another ban and once more depriving him of his office.[4] This time the papal edict proved of less success and Henry found himself in a stronger position. Sentiment in Germany was rallying in his favour. He replied to the papal ban by deposing Hildebrand. He accused him of countless crimes, ambition, avarice, simony, and sorcery and he set up a rival Pope. By a happy circumstance for Henry in a battle in which he was hard pressed by the armies of his rival, Rudolph, the latter was slain and an apparent defeat was turned into a victory. Henry, now the sole ruler of Germany, was in a position to reverse the humiliation of Canossa. He resisted every compromise of the Pope, and swept down into Italy. Although it took him three years, he finally conquered the city of Rome and on Palm Sunday, 1084, he had a rival antipope, Wibert, enthroned in Saint Peter's. On Easter Sunday of the same year Henry was crowned Emperor by Wibert. Meanwhile Hildebrand, taking safety in the castle of Saint Angelo, found his supporters deserting him, while the populace hailed the victorious German ruler. Henry finally left for Germany, never to return to Rome. Gregory then called to his aid the Norman armies from the South. These bold adventurers pillaged and ravaged Rome to such an extent that, although

---

[4]He sent Rudolph a crown with the inscription, *"Petra dedit Petro: Petrus diadema Rudolpho,"* once more claiming the papal right to appoint no less than to depose Emperors.

the Pope regained the possession of the Lateran Palace, he was forced to withdraw from the city of desolation and died in exile in Salerno.

The fate of Henry IV was no less tragic. Five years after the death of Hildebrand he revisited Italy and the success of his Italian campaigns was only checked, when he was driven back from an ill-fated attempt to besiege Canossa. The following year his reckless and headstrong son, Conrad, revolted against him. Long years of civil conflict both in Italy and Germany finally forced from Henry his abdication, in favour of his younger son (Conrad having died three years before). Harassed to the end of his days by the intrigues of his own family and by the Saxon revolts, Henry died in 1106. The enmity of the Church denied rest even to his dead body, which for some years lay in unconsecrated ground. But the long conflict of Church and State was far from ended. The spirit of Hildebrand lived on in his successors and the German kings demanded, no less insistently than Henry IV, the right of lay investiture.

The long warfare of the two powers through medieval history resulted in a series of compromises, the most important of which was sealed at the Concordat of Worms, where in 1122 it was agreed that clerical elections should be both ecclesiastical and secular. The candidate was in the first instance to be chosen by the Church, but the prince had the right of veto on any appointment. While the Church invested the priest with his staff and ring, the symbols of spiritual authority, the lay power invested him with the temporalities, the lands and wealth which were attached to the ecclesiastical office.

The problem which we face today is different from the medieval one. This is largely due to the rise of modern secularism which denies the ultimate rule of God over the State, deriving authority by a democratic process from below, rather than from above. Our relation is much nearer to the Church of the early centuries than to that of the Middle Ages. Our warfare is with god-defying states rather than with those that defend and uphold the Church. Even the so-called liberal, democratic states which allow the freedom of worship think of religion more as a harmless pursuit of a few than in any way the vital concern of the government. They are not openly allied with Christianity as the ultimate meaning of political life and follow the direction of the churches only when a successful lobby for some ethical legislation forces an issue upon them.

Yet the fate of medieval culture holds out a warning to us that the Church is not the State, and the presumptuous claim of the papacy to dictate in all matters to the secular power is fraught with danger to the true interests of the Church. It so involves the Church in the temporal situation that it robs it of perspective to transcend it. It can never voice the judgment of God upon an age and culture, which is its prophetic mission. While the nature of the necessary compromise between the Church and the Christian State is not a concern of the immediate present, we need none the less to be aware of the dangers involved in the medieval answer. For, as Christians, our own alignment with secular powers is open to the same tragedy of espousing a political cause and giving it the absolute sanction of religion.

Only once during the medieval period, was the attempt made to solve the problem by the suggestion that the Church should renounce its temporal possessions altogether, and so be free of any secular interference. This was put forward by Pascal II at the Concordat of Sutri, in 1111. It was a solution impossible for the Middle Ages. It would have reversed the development of medieval culture and deprived the Church of the means, by which, from the early days of the papacy, its spiritual decrees had been made effective.

The complete separation of Church and State, which such a theory entailed, is an idea with which we are familiar today. Yet it entails difficulties. It deprives the State of spiritual direction and makes the Church impotent to exert practical influence. Temporal power, in whatever manner it is conceived, in property or votes, is involved in the Church's existence in the world. To deny this is to set up a false division between spiritual and secular, between eternal and temporal.

We thus seem to be faced with a paradox. Temporal power involves the Church deeply in the social order and hinders its prophetic mission. Yet, if the Church possesses no temporal power, it is not involved enough in the world to be effective. Perhaps to realise the dilemma is halfway to its solution. On the one hand, this will prevent the Church calling any social order divine, and, on the other hand, it will help to avoid that error which conceives of the Church's mission purely in terms of the Hereafter.

THE CHURCH IN WORSHIP

What the Church meant in this epoch cannot be fully appreciated without some account of the Mass, which was the centre of the religious life of the Middle Ages.[5]

The claims of the Church to have the keys of heaven and hell, and to exercise power over princes and peasants alike, rested upon the medieval interpretation of the Mass. There the priest, vested with the supernatural authority of his office, mediated between man and God by re-enacting the divine drama of salvation on

[5]The word is derived from the concluding words of dismissal in the Latin Eucharist, *Ite missa est, missa* being a late Latin word for *missio,* dismissal.

Calvary. He called down God from heaven and in the form of a wafer sacrificed Him again for the sins of the world. The Protestant imagination is outraged by such claims, while the historian is awed by the fact that men believed them. For the medieval world the miracle of the Mass was no idle tale or superstition. If it was the source of the Church's spiritual and temporal power, it was no less the ground of salvation for the medieval world. In the Mass God was most near to the Christian. Though we may look askance at the superstitions which surrounded medieval devotion, we cannot deny the religious power that the Mass had for those generations. The medieval mind may have tended to regard everything in the concrete, to take the symbol for the reality, to identify the visible forms of the sacrament with its inner meaning. None the less, the vitality of medieval religion found its deepest expression in the Mass, where God stooped to share His life with sinful man.

The medieval Mass was distinguished by a very elaborate ceremonial, every incident of which was symbolic, in the same way that the structure and sculpture of the cathedral mirrored the whole life of Christian faith.

At the end of the procession and clad in his rich vestments, the bishop enters from the sacristy, representing Christ's entrance into the world from the Virgin. The two acolytes who precede him are the Law and the Prophets, while the four men who bear his canopy are the four Evangelists. At the opening part of the service the bishop is silent, as Christ was silent during his early years. The reading of the Epistle typifies the acknowledgment of Christ by John the Baptist. When the reader has concluded he bows to the bishop and so represents the Baptist humbling himself before Christ. The elaborate symbolism reaches its height in the central act of the Latin Mass, the elevation. Every incident in the preparation of the bread and wine for the communion is interpreted with reference to the journey of Christ to Calvary. When the bishop lays his hands over the elements and signs them with the cross, he represents the actual scene of the Crucifixion and the laying of the sins of the world upon the Holy Victim. Finally, when he repeats the words of Christ, "This is My Body," and "This is My Blood," he changes the inner reality of the bread and wine into the Body and Blood of Christ, sacrificed for the world. He holds them up to the congregation to be adored as the very presence of God among his people. It is at this moment of the elevation that the Mass reaches its height. The corporate sense of offering and participation in the Lord's Supper tends to give way to acts of individual piety and devotion in the adoration of the consecrated elements. The laity scrambled to witness the great moment in the service. If they failed to see the elements raised they imagined they had not heard Mass properly and waited for another. An English writer at the time of the Reformation says, that if the elements were not held high enough "the rude people of the country will cry out to the priest: Hold up, Sir John, hold up. Heave it a little higher." The origin of the ringing of a bell at this point in the service seems to have been to call the people in from the fields to witness the elevation while the priest had said the rest of the Mass practically alone. This individualism of late medieval piety was something against which the Reformers revolted. They wanted to restore the corporate sense of worship in the Eucharist by having all Christians partake of the Lord's Supper. It was a rare thing for the laity of the Middle Ages to communicate more than a very few times a year: the minimum requirement of the thirteenth century was once a year at Easter.

This general tendency reaches its height in the cult of the

Reserved Sacrament. Individual devotions are paid to the consecrated elements placed in an elaborate tabernacle, where they can be seen and adored at all hours. Communion is given before or after Mass from this tabernacle and becomes not a corporate act of worship but a highly individualistic form of piety. Yet it would be wrong to overemphasise this trend. While the parish Mass remained the central Sunday service and men could speak of Christendom as a living reality united in the single papal Church, there was always a sense of corporate Christian life and worship.[6]

In the symbolism of the Early Church and of the Middle Ages, the inner likeness of the symbol to the reality it represented is stressed, rather than its formal difference. This tendency to see things in the concrete reaches its climax in the medieval conception of the consecrated elements. They are no longer bread and wine in their inner reality; they have become the Body and Blood of Christ. To some it may seem that this is magic and superstition of the crudest type. Such an interpretation will miss the full significance of the medieval Mass.

The question to be asked is: What is the most real thing in this act of devotion? All Christians will answer: The Presence of Christ. The bread and wine and all the rest of the symbolism are but material channels through which God works and His abounding power and love in Christ are made real to us. So it was in the medieval Mass. The basic reality was the Presence of Christ, which was mediated through the consecrated elements. In the philosophy of the Middle Ages the attempt was made to distinguish the inner reality of a thing from its apparent form

[6]It is noteworthy that while this individualism long marked the Roman Mass and the faithful were accustomed to make their own acts of devotion by the use of private manuals and the rosary, the modern Catholic Liturgical Movement has made great strides in recovering the sense of corporate worship and offering which was characteristic of the Early Church.

or manifestation. The one had the technical term of "substance," the other of "accident." When applied to the Mass this doctrine was known as transubstantiation. It had been formulated as early as the ninth century by Paschasius Radbert, but while generally believed through the Middle Ages was not defined as an authoritative dogma until the thirteenth.[7] The substance of the sacrament remained no longer bread and wine but had been changed to the Body and Blood of Christ. The elements maintained their apparent and outward forms but their inner significance was something altogether different. The believer beheld in faith not bread and wine, but Christ. Transubstantiation was thus an attempt to give a philosophical foundation to the vital Christian experience, which we have already studied in the Eucharist of the Early Church. Like every such effort to explain the deepest religious experiences with the precision of philosophy and logic, it stood in danger either of petrifying them or of leading to superstition.

The general medieval tendency to regard everything in the concrete led easily to this second danger. In the rarefied atmosphere of scholastic learning the distinction between accident and substance might be apprehended, but to the popular imagination there was a vivid and miraculous change in the elements, which was often understood from the point of view of magic rather than of religion. That was the degradation of the Mass and the multitude of stories in which medieval literature abounds gives ample evidence that the general religion of that period was not of the high level which some modern enthusiasts for the Middle Ages would have us imagine. Monks recount fables in which they see an actual baby being sacrificed by the hand of the priest, and medieval writers in all seriousness record such remarks

[7] At the Fourth Lateran Council under Pope Innocent III, 1215.

as this (spoken of Peter of Brabant), "Peter devoureth little children, for I have seen him eat one at the altar." We may not wonder, therefore, that the Reformation came and the Reformers regarded the Roman Mass as nothing but superstition and blasphemy.

What, however, the medieval Mass always maintained was its objectivity. This has been something lacking in much Protestant worship. The Mass was an *actio,* a living drama constantly re-enacted for the salvation of men. The very realism of the medieval mind helped to keep this important point central. Worship was not "having a religious experience," it was traffic and communion with the Living God. It was the recognition of His condescension to man in Jesus Christ and at its best it was an act of offering in which Christians gave themselves to God and received the divine Life through the continued presentation, by the priest, of the sacrifice of Calvary.

THE CHURCH AND THE MONASTIC IDEAL

In its origins the monastic movement was a revolt against the corruption into which the Church fell after its recognition by the Emperors. The fact that the new religion was not only tolerated but granted privileges led to a consequent relaxation of its primitive moral rigour and earnestness. Moreover, the increasing chaos of the West, with the decline of the Empire, brought with it a sense of futility and despair about the normal course of affairs. The monastic movement offered men a new opportunity to cultivate the religious life. Unharassed by the cares of the world and the pressing obligations of ordinary life, the lonely hermit in the desert could devote himself to communion with God. Gradually the isolation of the hermit gave way to a more corporate sense of the monastic calling, and small groups of ascetics joined in a common life of discipline and devotion.

Asceticism can be understood in two ways. It can be cultivated because of a fundamental belief that matter is evil. The soul in its flight to the Divine has to be freed from the trammels and passions of the physical body. This is the basis of Oriental asceticism and to a limited extent it affected Christian monasticism in the East. The idea, however, which was more true to the Jewish heritage of Christianity and which played a significant rôle in Western monasticism, was that of the subjection of normal passions and desires to a higher spiritual end.[8] It was not the idea that the body is basically evil that gave rise to the monastic movement. Rather was it believed that man could not live the truly religious life, surrounded by and immersed in the sinfulness of the world. He must extricate himself from ordinary society and so be free to devote his whole attention to God.

The saint who did most to introduce monasticism into the West was Jerome, who died in the beginning of the fifth century. He was the most learned scholar of his day. Of him the great Augustine once remarked, "What Jerome does not know, no mortal will ever know." Gloomy and choleric by temperament, a man who hated and was hated with cordial reciprocity, Jerome devoted himself to the severest ascetic disciplines in the desert. His knees, he tells us, were hard as a camel's from his constant praying, and his skin was black as an Ethiopian's through continual neglect. But the rigour of his life in these wastes was by no means an assurance against temptation. Even in the very places where scorpions and wild beasts were his companions he would find his imagination wandering to Rome and to the bands

---

[8]Originally asceticism meant training: the discipline, for instance, that an athlete underwent. In the same way it signified discipline for the spiritual life.

of dancing girls whom he had known in his earlier life. His pagan literary pursuits and the fine polish of his style with its biting and sarcastic invective likewise haunted him. On one occasion he was visited with a vision of the Judgment Seat. Asked who he was, he replied, "I am a Christian." The judge answered, "Thou liest, thou art a Ciceronian, not a Christian!"

Jerome laboured long to get the wealthy families of Rome to turn their villas into monastic retreats and in Palestine he founded several institutions. Many of his distinguished converts were patrician widows and virgins whom he excited to the extremest ascetic practices. He expounded the Scriptures to them and flattered their spiritual vanity with his graceful correspondence.

Jerome has left us many vivid pictures of the Church in Rome during his day. His revolt against the idleness and luxury of the Roman clergy explains much of his monastic fervour. In a letter he tells, for instance, of those clergy who seek office only in order to cultivate the acquaintance of society women. These fellows think of nothing but how to dress like dandies. They scent themselves, curl their hair, and walk on tiptoe if the road is wet, so as not to splash their fine shoes. Their fingers glitter with expensive rings. They are more like potential bridegrooms than clergy. He pictures one of them getting up so early and starting on his visits that he thrusts his old head almost into the bedrooms of sleeping ladies. If he sees a cushion or some table-cloth that takes his fancy he praises it, regretting he has nothing like it, till the lady finally gives it to him. He has a saucy tongue and affected manners. He dines well and never fasts. He has carefully groomed horses. He is an adept at scandal, inventing and exaggerating tales. Such pictures may be caricatures but they reveal the deep and earnest feeling that awoke the Puritan spirit in the Church. The monastic movement was largely a revolt against this laxity of the clergy.

Monasticism[9] lay at the heart of the Christianity of the Middle Ages. In their renunciation of the world and their subjection of natural desires and pleasures for the cultivation of the spiritual life, the monks were one of the most potent forces in medieval culture. It is wrong to imagine that Christianity shut itself up in the monasteries for a thousand years and abandoned the world to evil and decay. The truth is rather that the monasteries were the vigorous nerve centres from which there flowed the religious life and activity of the Middle Ages.

The monks held up an ideal of self-discipline for a spiritual end. "Are ye not," urged Saint Bernard, "already like the angels of God, having abstained from marriage?" Whatever may have been the evils into which the monastic life fell, certain it is that this renunciation of the world had a profound effect upon the medieval mind. It raised the Church above the world and the ties and obligations of ordinary life. By that very fact, it surrounded religion with a certain veneration and awe. It gave concrete expression to complete devotion to spiritual pursuits, and it provided an organised and practical way of life for those saints of God who desired to abandon everything for religion. It made possible countless lives of simple and pure devotion unhampered by the duties of the world.

The main duty of the monks was the recitation of the services (or Offices) of which, by the sixth century, there were some eight or nine during each twenty-four hours. Later on, however, these were said in groups and the number of actual services was reduced to three or four. Psalm singing, prayers, and the reading

[9]Originally the monastic movements were lay movements. Only later did it become the rule rather than the exception for monks to be priests.

of select passages of Scripture, formed the main structure of these devotions. The monks did not imagine that their life of self-abnegation had value only for themselves; they were not interested merely in the salvation of their own souls. The monastic ideal had a social reference. The monks represented the whole people in their devotions, and the merit and virtue of their religious life was available for the world. It was believed that the prayers and petitions they made for others had especial efficacy, because of their self-consecration. In a true sense the verse, John 17:19, could be applied to the monastic ideal at its best, "For their sakes I sanctify myself."

The monastic system, however, was fraught with many dangers. Immorality always beset the monasteries, because such an ideal was impossible to realise on any large scale. Furthermore, the veneration with which the monks were regarded proved an easy source of acquiring wealth. A monkish Mass, for which the laity would pay a sum of money at the offertory, seemed in the popular imagination to have more value than one said by a secular priest.

The monkish imagination fed on miracle, and the weirdest and most unedifying visions and revelations were the result of the unnatural life of the monastery. A typical example of the monastic mind can be seen in a story told by Peter the Venerable. An immense demon stands beside the bed of a monk and converses with two fellow angels of Satan. One of them asks him what he has been doing. He replies that his efforts to corrupt the monk have been quite unavailing, as he is so well protected with a crucifix and holy water and psalm singing. The other two demons then give an account of their activity. One has just forced the head of a monastery into sin, the other has led a monk to commit adultery. They bid this idle demon get to work. "Do

something, you idle fellow, cut off the monk's foot that is hang-
ing out of bed." At once the demon seizes an axe from under
the monk's bed. He is in the very act of cutting off his foot,
when Divine Providence interposes, and the monk quickly draws
in the imperilled member, escaping the blow.

This story is by no means the worst that could be found.
Rather is it typical. It shows the vivid imagination of the time
and the tendency to see everything in the concrete. It is realistic
in its conception of the demonic and of miraculous protection
and intervention. But its interpretation of religion verges on the
trivial and the absurd.

Yet the importance of the monasteries cannot be overestimated.
They were the centres of the papal power all over Europe. Because their primary concern was religious and not secular, and
because they were unhampered by the natural duties of married
life, the monks could divorce themselves from all territorial interests. They became the champions of the extreme papal claims,
for they clearly saw that the complete independence of the Church
would guarantee the monasteries and their wealth from secular
interference. They were indeed the spiritual armies of the papacy
and it was from the monasteries that the great medieval Popes
came. The destruction of these houses by the secular rulers that
broke with the papacy during the Reformation was essential, for
the monasteries were the life centres of the papal power.

Then, again, the monasteries were the centres of learning,
education, agriculture, and medicine. Monks were not concerned
only with the recitation of the Offices. They reared the great
cathedrals, copied manuscripts, built roads, cultivated deserts,
bred horses, and pondered on theology. In this they were largely
distinguished from the early monastic movements of the East,
where the tendency had been to cultivate individual piety by the

rigour of ascetic discipline or by lonely contemplation. What Saint Benedict of Nursia, who died in 542 A.D., did for Western monasticism in his famous Rule was to Romanise it. He gave it a social outlook: he forced upon it social obligation. Its religious life was to be essentially corporate and sane. Its virtues were to be those of duty and obedience. He deprived it of its unhealthy and introspective elements and introduced a rule of work and manual labour. Though each monk took a vow of perpetual poverty, the monastery was far from poor. It was to be a self-contained spiritual community, not dependent upon the outside world for its subsistence, but giving rather than receiving alms. In the medieval period the monastic house was both well-ordered and self-supporting. It had its own bake-house, mill, fishponds, cattle, and fields. It cared for its own sick and was a centre of wealth rather than of poverty. During famine it supported the hungry; during times of scarcity it fed the peasants. The great monastery would even entertain princes who found its table and its cellar almost royal. The accumulation of monastic wealth naturally tended to enervate its original religious vigour, and one order after another fell into the sins of luxury, ease, and self-indulgence. Yet whenever this happened, a new monastic reform would be born and the early austerity of the Benedictine rule would be recovered. The history of the Middle Ages is largely the history of these reforms, following one another in rapid succession. As the new houses grew in wealth and importance there would ensue a consequent spiritual decline and this would be the occasion of a new reform.

Two instances of this will suffice by way of illustration—the foundation of the Cluniac movement and of the Cistercian. The Cluniacs dominated the eleventh century as the Cistercians did the twelfth. Both came at a period of monastic decline and introduced a rigorous and austere reform which affected the whole tenor of Church life. From Cluny came three great Popes, and the high fortunes of the papacy in its contest with the Empire owe not a little to the vigorous moral and religious reforms championed by Cluny. But the riches and power of Cluny led to its decline and the reassertion of the primitive austerity came with Saint Bernard, the founder and abbot of the convent of Clairvaux. Under him, the Cistercian monks attained to eminence through their simple life and their religious fervour. Bernard arraigned the Cluniacs for their self-indulgence and loose talk. Their avarice and ostentation showed itself in their splendid buildings and vast lands, their hard treatment of the peasants on their farms, and above all in their table which was distinguished by its varieties of dishes and wines. Bernard writes, "Their veins are swollen with wine and the monk arises from table ready for nothing but sleep."

Yet a similar fate befell the Cistercians and the energy of religious devotion passed to the mendicant orders of Francis and Dominic. With the growth of the towns in the thirteenth century, they started the popular preaching movements to serve those whom the monastic foundations could never reach. Monasteries belonged to the agrarian era: the mendicant orders to the urban.

The effect of the mendicants upon the medieval church was very significant. Even more than the older monastic orders, the friars were the emissaries of the Pope. They vowed direct allegiance to the Apostolic See. Legend records that Innocent III, the foremost Pope of the thirteenth century under whom the papacy reached the height of its power, saw in a vision the whole structure of the Lateran Palace supported by these two monks, Francis and Dominic. The two orders more than any other factor aided the papacy in its warfare with the secular power and helped to establish its jurisdiction over the local bishops. Hence the papacy granted favour after favour to the mendicant orders, above all giving them the privilege of hearing confessions anywhere.

Nothing was more objectionable to the parish clergy than the invasion of their territory by these friars. Through the confessional they collected fees that normally would have accrued to the parish priests. The laity were always more ready to confess to strangers than to their own clergy who were well acquainted with them. When the friars preached they drew the people from the regular masses, depleting the offerings and disorganising the general parish life. Saint Bernardino, one of the great figures of the Franciscan order, had said, "There is not so much risk to the soul in not hearing the Mass than in not hearing a sermon."

Where the mendicant orders played the most important rôle was in stamping out heresy. The Crusades, that fruitless attempt to reconquer Palestine for the Western World, had brought trade with the Orient and contact with Eastern culture. There followed the growth of the cities and a certain freedom of thought, through the influx of ideas from Arabic and Greek sources. Men began to resist the dogmatic attitude of the Roman Church and, turning to private speculation, they adopted ideas which were at variance with the Roman orthodoxy. In the attempts to suppress heresy the Dominicans and Franciscans played a leading part. The great Spanish Inquisitor Torquemada, for instance, was a Dominican, and both these orders were the zealous champions of the crusade of Innocent III against the heretics of the south of France.

There was, however, an element in the Franciscan order which was a source of constant trouble to the papacy. Indeed, from its very foundation the Pope had shown a certain suspicion of the movement which seemed to threaten the basis of the papal Church. The vow of absolute poverty which Francis and his early followers took, together with the preaching of a simple gospel and the imitation of Christ, formed a strange contrast to the powerful wealth, the subtle theology, and the imperial jurisdiction of the Latin Church. It showed up the pretensions of the Church in the glaring light of simple sainthood. At first the Pope was unwilling to grant his blessing to the new movement. Innocent III, at the time of Francis' visit to Rome, was a man of 50, strong and vigorous. Great success had attended his resolute action in re covering the Church's authority after the days of his feeble pred. ecessor, Celestine III. Francis was a young man of 29. The Pope was amazed by the severity of the rule that he had undertaken. He had vowed to follow the commandments of Christ with implicit obedience, throwing away staff and purse and shoes (Matt. 10) and being wedded to his bride Poverty, to whom he was devoted with all the pure chivalry of a medieval knight. Moreover, Innocent III warned Francis and his companions how impossible such a course of life would be. It seemed the wildest fanaticism to take Christ's counsels of perfection literally. Only after one of his cardinals, John of Saint Paul, had pointed out that the Church would be convicted of blasphemy if "we hold that the observance of gospel perfection is an irrational and impossible innovation," was he finally prevailed upon to bless the movement. The fact that no papal bull attended this decision may lead us to suppose that the Pope thought the simple and almost fanatic fervour of these men would be short-lived.

The spirit of Saint Francis has captivated the Christian imagination ever since. He has become the symbol of pure and Christlike humility and devotion. The Franciscan movement gave a new direction to Christian thought and to Church life in the following centuries. The conception of Jesus as the humble carpenter of Nazareth whose counsels were to be followed with simple devotion, was the beginning of Christian humanism. The figure of Christ was given a new interpretation. He was the servant of all, the perfection of obedience to God and simple humility, not the stern and unrelenting Judge of the medieval imagination. Along with this profound change came the growth of the various social and humanitarian movements of the following century, a new religious influence on Italian art, and above all the attack on the Church's wealth. Men who had come to feel the quickening touch of this Christ of the Gospels were outraged by the luxury and power of the medieval Church.

From the Franciscan movement sprang those extreme developments which demanded that the Church should renounce all wealth and in complete poverty devote itself to spiritual affairs, such as prayer, preaching and teaching. The papacy had shown shrewd wisdom in binding to itself this movement that might so easily have made a schism and caused the papal organisation untold trouble. Yet it could not altogether avoid the implications of the Franciscan ideal. It was left for Pope John XXII (in the fourteenth century) to utter anathemas against the extreme radical parties which grew from the Franciscan movement. In their contention that the possession of any property by the Church was contrary to the example of Jesus and essentially sinful, they were a source of constant trouble for the papacy.

The extreme Franciscans came to be known as the Spirituals, and they took over much of the teaching of the monastic seer Joachim of Flore. This prophet in three famous works which were later collected under the title *The Eternal Gospel,* understood history as the development of three successive periods, the last of which was soon to reach its consummation in a spiritual Church, committed to the Eternal Gospel or Gospel of the Kingdom. This near approaching spiritual age would see the conversion of all mankind and would reveal the hidden revelations of the Gospel of Christ. It would be the age of a purified, spiritual Church, free from formalism and corruption. The clerical order would be superseded by monks ("the little ones of Christ"), devoted to the contemplative life.

This contrast between the spiritual Church of the new age and the Catholic institution cut at the very roots of the Roman conception. The papal contention that the hierarchy represented the infallible Kingdom of God on earth was challenged by these monks who claimed to be the heralds of a new spiritual Church. In the place of the Catholic emphasis upon the divine institution that mediated the grace of God, the Spirituals stressed the future Church, which would be composed only of spiritual men, consecrated to true religion and virtue.

The ideal of Saint Francis is not without its difficulties. Withdrawal from the world, whether in the simple and humble service of Saint Francis or in the less attractive form of the early hermits and the monastic communities, can never answer the perennial problem that confronts the Christian. There are saints of God who are called to symbolise the pure life of Christian perfection, but they are rare and free spirits. It is impossible to lay down a rule of perfection to be widely observed. The same is true of the ideal of the celibacy of the clergy which it was impracticable to enforce on any large scale, as the history of the medieval Church constantly witnessed. The ideal is not the law. The Church has to have its organisation, its property, and its power, in order that it may become effective in the world. It has to give, not only to receive alms, as Benedict of Nursia perceived. It cannot prey on the population and it must have effective means of reaching all men. It has to answer the problem of life, not to withdraw from it. It must know that it does not and cannot live the perfect life. While its inspiration may come from those whom God has called to be saints, it cannot insist upon the ideal of perfection as the law for all its members, or for all its clergy.

The strength and weakness of the Roman Church in the Middle Ages is well reflected in the theory and practice of Indulgences.

The one date in Church History which every student remembers is 1517, when Luther nailed his Theses against indulgences to the door of the Castle church in Wittenberg. His action was of momentous importance, and the date is rightly regarded as the beginning of the German Reformation.

In the early period of Christianity the Church punished certain grave sins by the imposition of a period of penance. The "lapsed," for instance, had to give evidence of their sincere repentance before their reconciliation with the Church could be effected. They were excluded from the Eucharist for a number of years and were only readmitted to the Church after they had made public confession of their sin. At first penance was not regarded as a debt paid to God to satisfy the strict amount of punishment incurred by the sin. Rather did early Christians regard it as a sincere expression of repentance which was demanded before sinners could be reconciled with the Church. The legalism of the Latin mind, however, tended to give penance a different meaning altogether and the idea arose that sins committed after baptism could only be atoned for by meritorious works. The grace and forgiveness won by Christ on Calvary was not effective for such sins. Baptism washed away a man's former transgressions. However, if he fell into sin after baptism, he had to pay to God the exact price of the debt incurred. In one of his treatises Tertullian outlines the various disciplines which win a suitable amount of merit with God to pay these obligations. They included fasting, feeding on bread and water, weeping, groaning, dragging oneself in humility to the feet of the priests, and above all the act of martyrdom which, like a second baptism, washed away all sin. It was this rigorous and legalistic system which made the early Christians view the act of baptism with the greatest fear and awe. Like the Emperor Constantine, who was only baptised on his deathbed, they delayed it as long as possible, fearing lest by sinning after baptism they would lose salvation.

It was out of this that the penitential system of the Middle Ages evolved. Penance was not regarded as an outward expression of repentance, but as a satisfaction for sin committed after baptism. The theory underlying the medieval practice, however, was more advanced than in the Early Church. A clear distinction was made between the eternal punishment due to sin and the temporal punishment which God requires to satisfy divine justice. Such satisfaction had to be made either in this life or in purgatory. The idea is typical of the Middle Ages. It combined the Christian view of forgiveness with the Latin legal sense of justice. Penance paid the temporal price for sin. While the merit, which Christ had won by His sacrifice and perfect obedience to God, could be transferred to man, it could only wipe out the eternal punishment due to sin. It is significant that in the Early Church absolution by the priest followed penance. In the medieval epoch, however, the procedure was reversed. Penance was no longer regarded as a sign of repentance, but as a temporal satisfaction of God's justice. Absolution assured man that God had wiped out the eternal punishment due to sin, but it could do no more. Man himself had to pay the temporal price by performing the penance that the Church stipulated.

In the course of time it became a practical impossibility for the Church to require the rigorous penances which had been demanded in the earlier period of Christianity. The custom arose of mitigating penance, and this was especially true when long sickness prevented one of the faithful fulfilling the due amount required. It was impossible, for instance, for a sick man to fast with the same rigour required when he was healthy. Penances came to be changed and this principle of transmuting and even relaxing them, underlies the medieval indulgences. An important Teutonic custom also exerted an influence. In German law everything had its fixed price. If a man murdered another he could atone for his crime by the payment of a sum of money corresponding to the social rank of the murdered man. In the same way penances became commuted in financial terms. The equivalent of a pilgrimage of ten years was an annual payment of twelve shillings. For one day of bread and water could be substituted fifty psalms said on the knees or twenty-six solodi in alms. In this way penance often fulfilled useful services for the community. Penitents helped to build the cathedrals and by their alms they supported the great works of charity in the Middle Ages. The inconvenience of going on the crusades was estimated so highly that this meritorious work was reckoned in lieu of all penance.

The sale of indulgences, however, is connected not with the exact commutation of penance but rather with relaxing and even remitting the temporal punishment for sin. The question was at once asked by what right the Church could do this. The answer was given in the doctrine of the Treasury of Merit, which was first formulated by Alexander of Hales in the thirteenth century. This doctrine is a striking example of the logical and legal mind of the medieval theologian. It was maintained that there was a

vast storehouse, in which the merit of the good works of the
saints, the Virgin Mary, and Jesus Christ, was locked away for
safekeeping. The saints did not need all this merit for themselves and hence it could be used for sinners who were in debt
to God. The idea was rooted in one of the finest and most potent
concepts of the Middle Ages. The medieval Church was always
conscious of the spiritual oneness of the Christian community.
The Church was an organic whole in which the faithful shared
their spiritual blessings with one another. The saints could transfer
the merit of their good works to those in need, and the wealth
of this treasure house was infinite and inexhaustible. The abundant
merit of Jesus Christ far exceeded the temporal debt incurred by
any human sin.

How could men get at this treasury? It was claimed that the
papacy, since it had the keys to heaven and hell, had also the
keys to this storehouse of merit. The Pope could grant to those
in need enough merit to pay their debt. In this way the divine
justice was not peremptorily swept aside; rather was the pauper
given the means to meet his obligations.

The way in which the Church dipped into this treasure house
and made available its riches was by the sale of indulgences.
These could be purchased for nominal sums, graded in a kind
of tariff according to social status. Men bought them eagerly, for
they offered a complete assurance of satisfying the justice of God.
Sometimes the indulgences stated that a definite number of years
in purgatory[10] would be cancelled from the offender's debt: at
other times they offered plenary indulgence or complete release
from all temporal punishment for sin. Christians could never be
sure they had confessed all their sins; they were often in doubt

[10]Years in purgatory did not mean actual years but the purgatorial equivalent of
a given number of years of canonical penance on earth.

that the priest had meted out to them the amount of necessary
penance. Other sins of a grave nature they may not have chosen
to confess, fearing the long and severe penance they merited.
Furthermore, their friends may have died in sin and the purchase
of an indulgence could relieve their punishment in purgatory.
For all these reasons the indulgences seemed a great boon to the
medieval Christian. They meant forgiveness and remission of
punishment. The medieval man probably did not meditate deeply
upon theological questions or distinguish between eternal and
temporal punishment. Thousands of years in purgatory may have
seemed very like eternity. Indulgences, he believed, wiped out
the tragic consequences of sin and relieved him from the nightmare of punishment in purgatory. Hence their sale was a flourishing trade.

The papacy was not slow to realise the financial assets of this
traffic and we may sometimes wonder whether the papal treasury
or the Treasury of Merit was of more significance in the business.
It certainly did become a source of graft and the Roman Catholics
no less than the Reformers were not slow to point out the abuses
of the indulgence system. Pope Innocent III himself tried to
limit their sale and to put a check upon the cupidity of the clergy
who in the earlier Middle Ages had often sold indulgences without the permission of Rome.

One of the greatest scandals in this traffic concerns the sale of
the indulgence against which Luther wrote his Theses in 1517.
His protest was made on purely theological and religious grounds,
for he was quite unaware of the unholy compact that underlay
this particular sale. It has come to light only of recent years and
it may be of interest to recount it, since it evidences the kind of
corruption in the Roman Church which precipitated the Reformation.

It seems that an ambitious young noble (he was then only twenty-three), Albert of Brandenburg, who was already Archbishop of Magdeburg and acting Bishop of Halberstadt, was anxious to secure the arbishopric of Maintz, a wealthy see which had the added attraction of carrying with it an electoral vote.[11] The young man had managed, in a not too creditable way, to get himself elected by the chapter; but he was ineligible both on the grounds of age and of holding more than one see. In order to gain his purpose he tried to obtain a special papal dispensation and though the Pope, Leo X, at first hesitated to override so many canons of the Church, he was finally persuaded to screw up his conscience for the sum of ten thousand ducats plus the usual fees. Albert was in need of ready money and had to borrow the sum from the papal bankers, the Fuggers. The question naturally arose how he could pay off this heavy debt and to his joy the Roman Curia suggested a simple and ingenious method. A sale of indulgences would be started, ostensibly for the building of Saint Peter's in Rome, which Leo's predecessor, Julius II, had begun. But it was agreed that the young noble would push the sale in his dioceses and take half of the proceeds to pay off his debts. The other half was to go presumably to the building of Saint Peter's. Of course not a word of this bargain appeared in the papal bull declaring the indulgence. It merely stated in pious and extravagant language that those who took occasion of the offer could obtain full and complete remission of all their sins.[12] They could choose their own confessor, which meant they need not confess to their parish priest and acquaint him with sins of which they would rather he remain ignorant.

[11]A vote for the election of the Emperor.

[12]There were a very few grave exceptions and notorious sinners had to make public profession of penitence and receive three stripes of the scourge before getting full absolution.

The indulgence was just as effective for the dead. Friends and relations suffering in purgatory could be relieved of their torments immediately, if some kind cousin paid the appropriate price.

To Albert was committed the sale of the indulgences and he named a number of commissioners. One of these was the famous Tetzel, a Dominican friar, whose brisk trade in Jüterborg, not far from Wittenberg, provoked the protest of Luther. Tetzel seems to have been a fiery and eloquent preacher and a man of some learning. His popular presentation of his subject brought him both reputation and sales. He painted lurid pictures of dead relations suffering in purgatory, crying for help. Could his hearers remain adamant and callously abandon these poor suffering souls when such a small price could relieve their torments?

The sale of the indulgences was the occasion of great medieval ceremony. Tetzel himself was generally greeted with pomp. Solemn processions met him on his entry into the city. Flags, candles, and bells preceded him as he went to the Church and laid the papal bull on the high altar. Beneath the altar was set an iron chest to receive the contributions of the faithful and from this custom comes the couplet, mentioned in Luther's Theses:

"Sobald der Pfenning im Kasten klingt,
Die Seel' aus dem Fegfeuer springt."[13]

From this brief account it may be seen that the indulgences represent the strength and weakness of the Roman Church. There is no more profound conception than that the Christian fellowship is an organic whole, united in a single body, its members sharing spiritual blessings no less than temporal gifts. Nevertheless, the legalistic view of divine justice, the papal presumption which claimed to distribute the Treasury of Merit and the cor-

[13]As soon as the penny jingles in the chest,
The soul springs from the fire of purgatory.

ruption which beset the indulgence sales, are a strange contrast
to so noble an idea.

On All Saints' Eve, October 31, 1517, a monk of medium
height, emaciated with care and study, so that you could almost
count the bones beneath his skin, nailed ninety-five Theses against
Indulgences to the door of the Wittenberg Castle Church. A
contemporary, Mosellanus, describes him as a man of extraordinary learning, fresh, clever, cheerful, ever at ease in society,
with a vast store of subjects of conversation. Such was Martin
Luther. When he entered the lists against the indulgence traffic,
he was quite unaware of the grave scandal that underlay this
particular sale. His protest was made on religious grounds and,
although in his later life he confessed that his mind was not then
altogether clear on the implications of the indulgence traffic, he
had arrived at some very definite convictions. He purposely intended to hit at the crass abuses of the medieval Church and the
false conception of religion upon which they rested. His main
contention was that God grants complete remission of sins to
every true penitent, and the believer in Christ has no need of
these papal pardons to be assured that divine punishment for
sin has been remitted. Indeed, to give money to charity and to
those in dire need is more the Christian's duty than to buy indulgences. The Pope's authority cannot extend to purgatory and
he has only the power to remit the penalties which are imposed
by him or by the canons of the church. Luther brings up a series
of popular questions that the laity directed against the system.
In doing so he reflects the close contact he had with ordinary,
simple German people. He asks, for instance, "Why doesn't the
Pope empty purgatory for the sake of the most holy charity,"
rather than for the sake of money to build basilicas?

Luther's Theses were not intended as a rebel's proclamation

against the papal system. They were directed to the reform of
the Church, and to clarifying an issue, which had long been
debated and about which many sincere churchmen had had their
scruples. In common with medieval academic procedure Luther
nailed up his Theses as a challenge to theological debate, hoping
thereby to advance the true cause of religion and of the Church.
But they issued in no peaceful, scholarly debate. They sounded
the clarion of the Reformation. They hit at an abuse which was
keenly felt, for it was something that touched the pockets as well
as the consciences of the Germans. They were aware that the
sale of indulgences provided the papal treasury with a handsome
income and secured the position of the Pope as an Italian
sovereign. The subject was not one purely in the realm of
theological speculation, but it had great practical implications.
It touched the man in the street. It aroused discussion about an
issue which had financial roots and pointed directly to the papal
corruption. Thus it quickly rallied German sentiment around
Luther's cause. It provided an excellent occasion for the expression
of German antagonism against Italian encroachment in the form
of papal taxes and pardons. Luther attacked the medieval Church
at its weakest point and so precipitated the Reformation.

The Theses on Indulgences were the beginning of more far-
reaching attacks upon the Roman system. They provoked from
the papal champions antagonism and anathemas instead of a
sincere desire for reform. In the early days of the struggle
Luther had had some hope that the Pope would set his house
in order, but he was soon rudely awakened from this idle dream.
Within three years he was excommunicated by the Church, and
finally at the Diet of Worms he was placed under the ban of the
empire (1521). The warfare of Papalist and Protestant had begun
in earnest.

Luther's writings and actions were hardly calculated to produce peace. His was a stormy temperament. His sincere religious convictions could know nothing of compromise. His writings are full of reckless assertions, intemperate language, and bitter attacks upon his opponents. Yet they are no less marked by the profoundest religious discernment. He once wrote of himself, "I have no better work than indignation and zeal, for whether I want to compose, write, pray, or preach, I must be indignant." Such was Martin Luther, the violent but courageous champion of the Reformation.

THE SECTS AND THE INQUISITION

The claims of the Roman Church did not pass unchallenged during the Middle Ages. Opposition to the spiritual domination of the papacy was voiced by a variety of sects in Italy and South France at the very moment when the Church reached the height of its power. These anti-churchly sects sprang from many diverse traditions and their religious enthusiasm was often only a single element in very complicated social and political movements. The one factor which the dissenting bodies in the Middle Ages had in common was their determined opposition to the Roman hierarchy. Some of these sects, like the Waldenses, were purely religious, representing the Biblical evangelists of that era: others, like the Cathari in Southern France, gave religious expression to a movement that had its roots in the growth of an independent social and economic culture. Others again were but short-lived attacks on the corruption of the Roman Church by fiery enthusiasts, whose outbursts against its wealth and superstition were quickly suppressed.

The Church met these movements with a clear and vigorous policy. It stamped them out with the aid of the secular arm.

Resting back upon the theory of Augustine that the State must support the Church and advance its interests, the papacy instituted the Inquisition, by which heretics were tried, condemned and given over to the secular power for punishment. The death penalty by burning alive was generally enforced, though the Emperor Frederick II allowed the option, to be exercised by the judge, of having the tongue torn out. Confessions were extorted by torture. Princes refusing to co-operate with the Church were treated as heretics. Those who returned to the faith from fear of punishment were condemned to lifelong imprisonment. The property of heretics was confiscated: generally it passed to the State though there are instances of a division between the State and the Church.

The cruelty of the papal Inquisition, which flourished particularly in Spain, Southern France, Italy, and in German centres like Strassburg and Cologne, has often been enlarged upon. The underlying theory of the Inquisition, however, deserves some attention. The Church believed it was acting in the interests both of Christian society and of the heretics themselves, and it is true to say that the Inquisition at its best was not moved by cruel and barbaric spite. Inquisitors believed that eternal damnation would assuredly be visited upon the souls of heretics. Their execution, after every opportunity by persuasion and torture had been given for them to recant, was a social necessity, in order to prevent their luring others away from the Faith. When eternal salvation was at stake the Church tried to frighten heretics into submission by the fear of excommunication, which involved death from the secular power. If they recanted, imprisonment was looked upon as a satisfaction for their sin, an opportunity for repentance, and a prevention against backsliding and the infection of others. If, on the contrary, they remained obstinate in their heresy, the Church excommunicated them and handed them over to the State. In accordance with established custom (since the fifth century), the secular power executed them as anti-social and unfit to belong to the body politic. By their heresy they denied the divine foundation of medieval society and were rebels against its highest law.[14] It was generally regarded that the Church's province extended no further than to excommunication, though various forms of punishment including imprisonment, but never execution, were looked upon as canonical measures of penance and atonement.

What was deplorable about the Inquisition was not its cruelty, in which it was the child of its age, so much as its presumptuous identification of the Roman hierarchy and decrees with the perfect expression of God's will upon earth. It gives us in the most vivid and dramatic form the dreadful consequences of elevating that which is human to the sphere of the divine, and confusing the judgment of man with the judgment of God. The same error besets every attempt to interpret the will of God in history and is no less evident in those extreme forms of political radicalism or conservatism which claim divine sanction. While man is forced to make absolute decisions in every aspect of his life in history, none of these can claim perfectly to embody the will of God. All stand under His judgment and are only redeemed in the fellowship that is born of the humility of repentance in Jesus Christ.

To illustrate these attacks upon the Roman Church the Cathari may be cited as an example. By the beginning of the thirteenth century they had grown strong in North Italy and South France, but they represent not a single unified movement but a variety of some fifty or more sects which shared a general outlook and

[14]On the whole such executions were only occasional in the West until the attempt of the Church to suppress the Cathari heresy in Southern France in the thirteenth century.

purpose. They were dominated by the idea of returning to the life of the primitive Church. Their criticisms of the papal hierarchy were drawn from a study of the Bible, which they tended to regard in a somewhat legalistic fashion as a book of minute regulations and prescriptions for conduct.

The movement was firmly rooted in the south of France, which had developed a flourishing culture that separated it from the rest of Europe. The growth of important towns, through the commerce stimulated by the Crusades, had brought with it a certain independent spirit, which expressed itself in the art, architecture, and luxury of southern France. The influx of Arabic and Eastern culture did much to stimulate this early Renaissance, which was marked by the development of medicine, the toleration of the Jews, and the carefree spirit of the Provençal troubadours. The general tenor of life in the warm climate of southern France contrasted with the temper of the North and of medieval Europe in general.

This independent spirit of the southern provinces showed itself in the religious sphere. The Cathari faith with its moral exclusiveness and its denunciation of the Roman Church spread with rapidity. By the end of the twelfth century it is said to have had over four million adherents. The two chief roots of its doctrine were an Oriental dualism of matter and spirit, and a very sectarian attitude toward the Church. The first of these was of Eastern origin and came into France through the contact of the West with the East in the Crusades. It entailed a fundamental denial of the development of Catholic Europe, where the tendency had been to regard the material world as participating in and reflecting the spiritual. To the Cathari such a belief was blasphemous. They held all matter to be basically evil and hence they preached the most rigorous asceticism. To refrain from marriage, to refuse all meat, eggs, and cheese were their counsels of perfection. Sexual intercourse was abhorred as the vilest sin, and to such an extent did they press their doctrine that faithful men were forbidden to sit on a bench with a woman, no matter how long the bench might be. Their belief entailed an attack upon the whole Catholic sacramental system as superstitious. With this Oriental religious philosophy was mingled a stern denunciation of the corruption of the Roman Church. Its wealth and property were regarded as essentially evil, and the moral conscience and Biblical literalism of the Cathari led them to oppose war in all its forms and to refuse oaths in civil courts. The perfect life was to be untrammelled by the earthly ties and obligations of civic life no less than of wealth, property, and marriage. Their self-detachment from the world was to be as complete as possible, and only that labour was permitted which was necessary to sustain life.

Among the Cathari there were two grades of believers. There were those who had almost wholly abandoned the material world and by their lonely isolation and their ascetic disciplines had conquered all material passions and desires. These *Perfecti*, as they were called, had the right to bear office in the sect, a privilege reserved only for those whose superior detachment from the world was attested by the rite of consolation (*consolamentum*). This rite, a kind of equivalent to Catholic baptism, was only granted to those who adhered to the strictest requirements, which included the renunciation of marriage and property, and demanded a diet which excluded all meat, milk, and eggs. It was conferred by the laying on of hands, and the placing the Gospel of Saint John on the candidate's head and it was regarded as the only valid apostolical succession. Women, as well as men, could receive and give it.

The *credentes* (or believers) were those who had not yet reached the stage of perfection. They were the majority of adherents and while they lived the normal life of the world and even maintained their attachment to the Roman Church, they were promised the rite of *consolamentum* on their deathbed. The *credentes* were the main support of the movement. Many of them belonged to the rich middle classes of Southern France and, as well as providing for the *perfecti,* they aided the movement by large grants of money for propaganda.

In their doctrine of the Church the Cathari were the heirs of the Donatist movement, holding that the true Church is the Church of the saints. The Christian community thus became, not the fellowship of the faithful, but the society of the morally perfect. The ethical life of the clergy was the guarantee of the validity of their ministrations. If they fell into mortal sin they could grant no effective *consolamentum,* and even those they had already given lost their validity. The grace of God was thus made dependent upon the perfection of man, and no one could be certain that the sacraments he received were valid and would continue to be so.

It cannot be denied that the moral vision of these sects was often more profound than those of the Church of that day. In their stress upon the equality of women and the renunciation of war they were in advance of their age, and their denunciations of the laxity and corruptness of the Roman clergy were not without justification. But they fell into the same error that frequently attends earnest moral reform. They limited the Church to those who conformed to their particular standards, and claimed that the grace of God depended upon man's merit. The theory has an interesting relation to the papal conception. Both give something historical and relative an absolute and divine significance. The Cathari deified ascetic perfection, while the Roman

Church deified an historical organisation. Furthermore, the ascetic conception of the Cathari was based upon a fundamentally un-christian attitude to the material world, which they regarded as basically evil and not as the creation of God.

The most bitter and successful attack upon this sect came with the crusade of Pope Innocent III and the institution of the Inquisition. Twenty years of warfare, in which the Pope and the King of France were united, brought the independent spirit of the southern nobles into submission, creating a centralised France. Little did the Pope, in the hour of his triumph, realise that the next century would witness this same united France virtually capturing the papacy and making it a French institution. Out of this finally grew the papal schism which more than any-thing else lowered the prestige of the Apostolic See, and so the rise of French nationalism hastened the downfall of the papal power in Europe.

CHAPTER V

THE ROOTS OF THE REFORMATION
OF THE CHURCH

THE roots of the Reformation are manifold. The Protestant revolt against papal authority does not represent a purely religious movement. Rather was religion one of the most potent factors in an upheaval which was grounded in every aspect of the national and social life of those countries which came to adopt Protestantism. An understanding of the religious issue will be gained only from a survey of those other forces which contributed to the Protestant revolt.

First among these is the assertion of national cultures. The unity of the Middle Ages was ecclesiastical, rather than political. It was superimposed by the Roman Church, which gave the Latin genius for law and organisation a Christian direction. Its success lay in the fact that it provided Europe with a centre of unity and religious meaning at the moment of its greatest need, when the barbarian invasions spread havoc and disorder. But it was doomed to inevitable failure; for it united two distinct and in many ways opposing elements—the Latin culture of the old Empire and the barbarian cultures of the North. For well-nigh a thousand years it maintained itself; but when the barbarian nations had had time to mature their cultures, the superstructure of the Latin Church was unable to resist their vigorous assertion. Thus were born the national states of Europe, which, conscious of their self-sufficiency, were determined to pursue a course independent of any superimposed religious unity. The Reformation, which started in Germany, derived not a little of its force and vigour from Luther's insistence that Germany had been a prey of Italian ecclesiastics and Italian taxation. "I am the prophet of the Germans," he confidently asserted. He rallied to his cause the new German sentiment, and provided the Teutonic consciousness with an independent religious expression.

It is interesting, moreover, that the great powers, which came to adopt Protestantism in one form or another as a national religion, lay outside the sphere of influence of the old Latin Empire. The Teutonic and Scandinavian countries with England and Scotland, revolted against the Latin elements which the Roman Church had assimilated. In a similar way the Bohemian movement under John Huss, which preceded the Reformation by a century, is to be understood as a national rising. It represented the Czech consciousness, in opposition to the encroachments of the German Empire in alliance with the papacy. It was different, however, with France, where the national consciousness had perhaps first developed. The alliance of French and papal interests had created a centralised France in the crusade against the Cathari. Finally, she had managed to capture the papacy itself, which during the seventy years of its captivity in Avignon virtually became a French institution. Furthermore, while the Gallican Church always tried to preserve a certain independence of the most extreme papal claims, the Latin influence was a great factor in French development and thus predisposed it to the Roman form of the Christian religion. A similar situation was true of Spain, where the conquest of the Moors and the unification of Spanish territory was vitally connected with the papal alliance and with the Inquisition.

If the revolt of the North represented the awakening consciousness of the barbarian element in medieval culture, the

Renaissance was an attempt of the Latin world to recapture its classical heritage. The revival of Greek learning through the contact of West with East in the Crusades reached a climax, when, with the capture of Constantinople by the Turks in 1453, the Greek culture was driven westward. Italy awoke to claim a lost inheritance and to cast off that alien tradition of Latin Christianity, which had rejected the free spirit of classical humanism and had imposed the rigid disciplines of medieval religion and piety. The men of the Renaissance fell in love with life, while their predecessors had been in love with religion. To express life and not to discipline it was their highest aim. The Gothic spirit seemed untutored and barbaric. The finiteness of man, expressed in that greatest achievement of medieval art, the stained-glass windows, with their rigid lines enclosing the saints in their ascetic perfection, was overthrown for the sense of man's infinite capacities. While the traditional religious names were given by artists to their pictures, they no longer painted medieval Madonnas, but they expressed the perfection of the human body with the same spirit with which the Greek had depicted Aphrodite. Instead of the religious and organic order of medieval Europe, the Renaissance stressed the individual with his capacities for emotion, feeling, and thought. The geographic expansion, with the discoveries of Africa and America, awoke men from the narrow parochialism of the Middle Ages: the earth seemed to hold treasures undreamt of, and luxuries and excitement to satisfy every human craving. Indeed, so overwhelmed were men with the new potentialities of human existence, that a sense of emptiness, a kind of *ennui* beset them. This is perhaps the true meaning of Dürer's picture *Melancholia*. They were like children with too many new toys. Life was too full to have any ultimate meaning. Religiously it became empty; it lost that firm

sense of spiritual direction and religious cohesion that had characterised the Middle Ages.

For a period, the Roman Church in Italy became imbued with
the Renaissance spirit. The Popes of the second half of the fifteenth
and early sixteenth centuries were celebrated more for their
patronage of the arts than for their religious devotion. With the
Borgia family (and especially with Alexander VI) the papal See
sank to its lowest spiritual and moral ebb. The Popes were essentially Italian princes, uniting literary and artistic tastes with
military and political ambition, and playing a crafty game in
the arena of Italian politics, in which intrigue and murder were
the order of the day.

In many ways the Reformation was a reaction against the
luxury and irreligion of the Renaissance. The great Reformers
were the champions of strict morality and a dominating religious
purpose in all life. Yet in two ways the Renaissance contributed
directly to the Reformation. Protestantism derived from it a
feeling for antiquity and for the infinite importance of the
individual. But to both these ideas it gave a religious meaning
not inherent in the Renaissance. Not classical antiquity, but the
antiquity of the Early Church was the ideal of the Reformers.
Ad fontes, "back to the sources," was their motto. They looked
upon the medieval years as the corruption of the Early Church.
They turned to the New Testament, and not to the canon law
and tradition of the Church, for their inspiration.

The stress upon individualism in classical Protestantism has
often been misunderstood. The Reformers were not the champions of isolated and individual piety. That was more characteristic of the late medieval Church with its cult of the Reserved
Sacrament. What the Reformers stressed was the corporate nature
of Christian life and worship, which comes from the recognition

that every human soul has direct access to the living God. They were opposed to the claim of the medieval Church that, by virtue of its divine authority, it mediated between man and God. They contended that every Christian was a priest and that by faith he could enter into the Holy of Holies. He did not need the assistance of an order of clergy, who alone claimed to have the right to approach God directly. The only assistance the Christian needed was that of the corporate body of believers who together worked and prayed to the glory of God, and together enjoyed the fruit of redemption in Christ Jesus. Classical Protestantism was not individualistic. While it recognised the infinite worth of the individual before God, it was emphatic upon the corporate nature of Christian life.

The Protestant attack upon the papacy was not only rooted in its revolt against the luxury and corruption of the Renaissance. Other circumstances had deprived the Apostolic See of the reverence with which it had been formerly regarded. Among these were the Avignon Captivity and the Papal Schism. From 1309 to 1377 the Popes had dwelt in France. The immediate cause of their removal from Rome had been the family feuds of the Orsini and Colonna in that city. The troubled state of Italian politics had endangered the very lives of the Popes. In their retirement they found peace and security under the ægis of the French power, but their prestige was greatly lowered. All the Avignon Popes were Frenchmen and it seemed that the papacy had become a French institution. On their return to Rome a fatal schism broke out, due to the same family feuds and the French and Italian rivalries to capture the papal throne. On the death of Gregory IX (1378) the Cardinals first elected a man Urban VI, who began to pursue a course of staunch antagonism to the French influence. This provoked hostility from rival quarters, and the Cardinals, four months after the election, were forced to reverse their decision. They now chose Clement VII who almost immediately took up residence in Avignon. Urban refused to abdicate, and Europe was confronted with the travesty of two Popes. Through medieval history there had not infrequently been rival claimants for the Apostolic See. What was shocking about this schism was that it had been caused by the Church itself. It was not a case of an emperor setting up an antipope. The Church itself had brought to birth this "twin-headed monster," as a contemporary called it.

For nearly forty years the schism lingered on. When the rival Popes died, the Cardinals of the two factions named their successors. An ill-fated attempt to heal the schism was made in 1409 at the Council of Pisa, but it only resulted in the creation of a third Pope. Not till 1417 was the peace of the Church once more restored and a single Pope (Martin V) universally recognised by all Christendom.

A new theory of authority had been born. The medieval contention that no one on earth is superior to the Pope had been displaced by a conception of a general council which could make and unmake Popes. Although the medieval theory was again restored and reached its height in the definition of papal infallibility in 1870, irreparable harm had been done. The more democratic theory of a limited papal monarchy was upheld by such theologians as Jean de Gerson. The full implications of the democratic position, that political and ecclesiastical authority are delegated from the people and not devolved through Pope and Emperor, were worked out by Marsilius of Padua. Of these ideas Calvin, and to a lesser extent Luther, were the inheritors.

In the theological realm the Reformation was an effort to do away with the vast and complicated system of medieval religion and to get back to first principles. The scholastic theologians had expended their efforts in building a comprehensive scheme of theology and religious practice, which dealt with every phase of Christian life and faith in infinite detail. The fine and subtle distinctions they made in their thinking often did more credit to their unwearying logical precision than to their religious insight. While the Reformers challenged the very foundations upon which this superstructure had been reared, not a little of their success came from the fact that the Church's laws and theology were so complicated and obscurantist. The revival of classical learning had driven men back to the sources of the Christian religion. The simplicity of the Gospel contrasted vividly with the mass of medieval superstition that went under the name of Christianity. Scholars, like Erasmus, laboured to expose the follies of stupid monks and unlearned clerics, and advocated that the articles of belief should be reduced to the fewest and simplest. They criticised the adoration of relics. They strove to recover the writings of the Fathers of the Early Church so that men could venerate the saints and not their old slippers. Simple and enlightened faith was to take the place of medieval ignorance and superstition. Historical inquiry had shown that many of the claims upon which the Roman Church rested its primacy and jurisdiction were false. The document, for instance, known as *The Donation of Constantine,* which recorded that the Emperor on removing the seat of imperial power to the East had donated to the Pope the temporal authority of the Western world, was proved by Laurentius Valla on the grounds of its Latin style to be a forgery of the ninth century.

Something of what this meant can be gathered from the *Epistles of Obscure Men,* a series of imaginative letters which appeared in Germany from the pens of two Renaissance humanists.[1] They hold up the scholastic system to heartless ridicule. They are extremely clever and, though they exaggerate the Church's abuses and follies, they contain that element of truth which makes them really biting. In one of them a certain Heinrich Schafmaul writes to a learned cleric demanding help on a knotty problem in theology. He tells how he went with a friend to an inn and ordered an egg. When he opened it he found a chicken inside. He asked his comrade what he should do. He replied, "Eat it up quickly, for if the manager sees it he will charge you for a fowl, and there is a rule in this house that you have to pay for whatever is put on your table. What is more, he will charge you for a fowl no matter how small it is." Heinrich ate it up. Then conscience troubled him. He remembered it was Friday. He had committed a mortal sin by eating flesh on Friday. His friend urged on the contrary that it was not even a venial sin, as a chicken counted only as an egg till it was born. It was the same with the little bugs in cheese and vegetables which one generally ate in taverns, and it was only the landlords who called them flesh in order to get a high price for their food. Well, he pondered on the problem thinking over how a learned doctor had told him that the grubs in cheese counted as fish, whereas young chickens in eggs seemed more like meat. So he wrote to the learned Magister demanding advice. He was especially anxious to know if the sin was mortal, so he could get absolution in Italy before returning home to Germany—a sly thrust at the easy way one could get forgiveness in Rome.

Such a state of affairs must not be overemphasised. There is

[1]These were published anonymously and were probably written by Crotus and Von Hutten. The title of the letters was itself satirical. The letters purported to be a defense of the clergy and monks against the attacks of the humanists, especially of Reuchlin, the famous Hebrew scholar, who, to offset the defamation of scurrilous monks, had collected some testimonies from eminent men to his scholarship. These he published under the title, *Letters from Eminent Men.*

another side to the picture, represented by those popular movements in religious education which the Church had undertaken
since the thirteenth century. In practically every land the Church
had tried to enforce a knowledge of the *Pater Noster,* the *Credo,*
and the Ten Commandments, as a minimum for all the faithful.
The fifteenth century saw an ever-increasing number of cate-
chetical and devotional manuals for popular use and instruction.
Many of these were written in verse and illustrated, and they
paraphrased in simple and pointed language the Ten Commandments and the main articles of the faith. The medieval service
of Prone is of equal importance. Although the liturgy itself was
said in Latin, a little vernacular service of prayer and instruction
was inserted before or after the sermon. Here the people learned
the Lord's Prayer and heard the Psalms and Collects in their
own tongue. This preparation of the laity was a very significant
factor in the success of the Reformation. Luther had a deep
understanding of the simple people and always kept closely in
touch with the peasant and artisan of his native Germany. When
he called them back to what he imagined was primitive Christianity and spoke to them in the simple language of the Creed
and the Ten Commandments, their response was immediate
because their understanding had been prepared. Most of them
were already versed in the great fundamentals of the Christian
religion. All significant revolutionary movements in history are
preceded by periods not of darkness, but of enlightenment. The
Reformation drew its vigour and success from the fact that the
people could understand that the Church was obscurantist, because they knew something of what it ought to be.

Another root of the Reformation lies in the popular mystical
movements of the late fourteenth and fifteenth centuries. In the
Netherlands, the Rhineland, and Southwest Germany, groups of

laity with some clerics banded together in a semi-monastic life. While under common rules it was neither official nor bound with permanent vows. These brotherhoods were variously named Friends of God, Brethren of the Common Life, while the more extreme radical wing was known as Brethren of the Free Spirit. In their devotion they ranged all the way from simple churchly piety to a more extreme mystical pantheism that disregarded sacraments and institutions altogether. Their importance lies in their educational activity, particularly in such centres as Deventer, where Erasmus was educated, and in their stimulation of inward spiritual religion. Some of this was undoubtedly individualistic and other-worldly, but its simple devotion to Christ and its powerful spirituality can be seen in its foremost classic, the *Imitation of Christ*. Some of its literature had a profound effect on the Reformers. Luther, for instance, was influenced by the sermons of John Tauler, whose denunciations of external ceremonies and of reliance on good works foreshadowed the Reformation. This mystical movement was an important break with the medieval system, because it did not presuppose the whole churchly superstructure which claimed to be the only approach to God. Rather did it find Him in the simple devotion of the penitent heart.

One final word must be said about the philosophic system which paved the way for the Reformation. This was Nominalism, a fundamental revolt in the fourteenth century against the thinking of the earlier scholastics. Its presuppositions were the reverse of those on which the medieval superstructure had been reared. Realism,[2] the predominant philosophy of the Middle Ages, was based on the idea that what is ultimately real is not the particular and individual things we see and touch, but rather the hidden

---

[2]This must not be confused with modern Realism of which it is almost the exact opposite. Medieval Realism is fundamentally allied to Platonic Idealism.

and universal truth behind them. The Church was not the local congregations added together, but The Divine Church in its transcendent meaning. The local congregations only became Church when and insofar as they participated in the Real Church, of which they were but the shadows and reflection. Similarly the Empire was viewed as an organic whole. It was not the apparent unity of the particular states of Europe. While this was the theory, the medieval tendency to see everything in the concrete led practically to identify the visible Church with its transcendent reality. Thus visible institutions were clothed with a divine significance and the extravagant claims that supported them were often unchallenged.

The Nominalists reversed this procedure. They claimed that what were most real were the particulars, the individual things, whereas the organic whole was only an idea[3] deduced from a consideration of a number of particulars. The Nominalist contention thus robbed the medieval world of its most profound meaning. There was no Church, no Empire, which participated and shared in the real and transcendent Whole. There were only individual churches and particular states.

The full implications of the Nominalist position were not clearly worked out, for along with this idea went a stern denunciation of human reason and the ability of man naturally to perceive and to understand the divine truths of revelation. The will of God appeared from the point of view of human understanding to be arbitrary, irrelevant to reason. The great Nominalist theologians, like Occam and Biel, used this theory to enhance the power and dignity of the Church, and to demand implicit and unquestioning obedience to its divine decrees. Yet it is obvious that the same system could be used to deny the Roman Church

[3] A notion, or name (*nomen*), whence the system was called Nominalism.

altogether. This is precisely what the Reformers maintained. God speaks His Divine Word to each individual soul and to the company of believers bound together by Faith. There is no need for a divine institution to mediate God's Word to man. He speaks directly to whom He will, and they who hear His call are knit together in a spiritual brotherhood that transcends the world.

Chapter VI

THE CHURCH IN THE LIFE AND THOUGHT
OF THE REFORMATION

INTRODUCTION

THE Reformation in its religious aspects represented both unity and diversity. It produced a great variety of conceptions of the nature of the Church and embodied them in many different organisations. Yet the Protestant churches were agreed in three fundamental convictions. In the first place, they held that the Roman Church was not the sole and infallible medium of God's authority in the world. The will of God was not revealed in any human institutions but was made known to men in the Holy Scriptures read by faith. The Bible became the final source of authority for Protestantism and although the Reformers differed in their interpretation of it they were at one in their belief that God speaks through it to the individual soul. The ultimate authority was not the Scripture as a barren record, but the Scripture read by faith, illumined and made alive by the Spirit of God.

Secondly, the Reformers denied the miracle of transubstantiation whereby the grace of God was limited to the sacrament and made dependent upon the action of a priest mediating between the people and God. Finally, the most profound insight of Protestantism lay in its insistence that the reconciliation of man with God was not determined by anything he did. It was not the work of man, but of God. Forgiveness could not be purchased by the merit of good works or by buying indulgences. It was the gift of God through Jesus Christ. What Christ had accomplished by His death and Resurrection had been accomplished once for all and was available for all men, who in penitence and in faith accepted this gracious gift of God. The Mass could not re-enact the sacrifice which Christ had made on Calvary. Christian worship could but proclaim what God in His infinite mercy had done in the sending of His Son. The Gospel of the Reformation was as simple as it was profound. The unconditional forgiveness of God through Jesus Christ was its basic theme. It released men from the haunting fears of purgatory, from the superstitions of the Mass, and from the presumptuous identification of the Roman hierarchy with the Church of God. It proclaimed to men freedom from the vast and complicated system of penances, merit, and indulgences. It gave them assurance of the divine forgiveness, when they were beset with doubts and were striving to win merit with God. It freed them from the trammels of the Church, with its laws, its decrees, and its penances.

It is perfectly true that the medieval liturgy, no less than much medieval theology, taught that man is only saved by the grace of God and can do no good work without His aid. Yet the tendency to stress man's ability to please God, rather than his sinfulness and complete dependence upon God, is apparent in the later scholastic theology. Occam, the Nominalist, for instance insisted that the powers of the human will were sufficient for man's self-renewal. Furthermore, the general teaching of the Church had been to interpret Christianity as a law rather than as a gospel. The self-discipline of the monastery was looked upon as meriting more favour with God than the normal vocations of life, while the conception of penance as the temporal satisfaction of divine justice involved the idea of man's ability to win merit with God. It was against this background that the Reformation stressed the abounding mercy of God and the impotence of man. The Reformers contended it was nothing but blasphemy and presumption on the part of the Roman Church to claim that it had divine authority to measure merit and penitence, and to dispense indulgences. With deep religious discernment Protestantism refused to regard anything human as divine. Ecclesiastical institutions were the erections of men, not of God. He made known His saving power only when He spoke His Word of forgiveness to the believing heart and to the people of God gathered to worship Him. The word of His power broke through all human and temporal institutions, condemning their corruption and the pride of man, upon which they were built. Yet at the same time the mighty Word of God proclaimed forgiveness and salvation to the repentant and humble sinner, who had only to accept His promise in faith and to know that God was all in all.

Such a gospel shook the foundations of medieval Europe. The ecclesiastical unity by which it had been held together for so many centuries was broken. The religious upheaval was associated with the spirit of nationalism, and there appeared independent princes and kings who were no longer united by a common religious allegiance. It is true that the Reformers believed secular authority to be commanded by God and many of them held that the temporal powers should preserve and defend the Protestant religion. Nevertheless, the basic medieval conception of the unity of Europe as an organic and corporate whole, founded and centred in the religious sanction of the Catholic Church, ceased to have any significance. Obedience to institutions might be commanded by God, but through no human institutions could He be said to reveal Himself. Thus Christendom passed away, and the Catholic and Protestant states of Europe were born.

There were four dominant conceptions of the Church which

the Reformation produced. There was first the Lutheran, in which the Church was regarded as the body of the faithful, the corporate society of those who had heard and received the word of God. Its organisation was of secondary importance. Its essential meaning was its foundation in faith, which was interpreted as the humble acceptance of God's forgiveness in Christ. Secondly, there was the Calvinistic position, in which the Church was viewed from two points of view. On the one hand it was the body of the elect, the unknown company of those whom God had chosen through the ages and throughout the world for salvation. On the other hand it could be regarded as an institution, distinguished by its preaching the doctrines of Holy Scripture and by its celebrating the sacraments of baptism and the Lord's Supper. To this institution God commanded the faithful to belong for the nourishment of their spiritual life. A third view was represented by Richard Hooker, the Anglican theologian. Like Calvin he distinguished between the company of the elect and the institution, but he tended to give the latter a national sense. While the Church in its temporal manifestation embraced believers all over the world, it was divided into distinct societies, each with its own ecclesiastical polity. Many of these societies were bounded by national territories and the Church could thus be regarded as the nation on its knees. Church and State were two aspects of a single society, and thus Hooker, in national terms, revived something of the medieval conception of the organic unity of society. A fourth idea of the Church was held by the Anabaptists. They claimed it was an association of believers, which was knit together by the symbols of the Eucharist and adult baptism, and truly represented the Kingdom of God in this world by its perfect justice and goodness. It was a foreshadowing of the Kingdom of Christ which would almost imme-

diately appear on earth. Some of the Anabaptists organised themselves into a kind of small religious-political state, independent
of the evil kingdoms of the world.

Luther's idea of the Church cannot be understood without
an examination of what he means by the Word. The Word of
God, he contends, is the personal manifestation to us of our
salvation. It is the power of God which enables us to grasp His
promises. It alone is infallible and authoritative. A man hears it
and he knows it is God speaking. There is no criterion in history
or reason whereby he can judge it. God speaks: man hears or
refuses to hear. The dynamic power of God breaks in upon
history, shatters human reason, condemns human presumption.
Yet at the same time it awakens faith in the penitent heart. It
speaks to man the assurance of salvation in Jesus Christ.

To Luther this dynamic Word of God was conveyed particularly through Holy Scripture. The Bible was not a collection of
correct propositions from which reason could make deductions
with the accuracy of logic. That was a scholastic idea of Scripture.
Nor, on the other hand, did Luther consider it a compilation of
inerrant statements of fact. That was the more Calvinistic view.
To Luther Scripture conveyed the Word of God. God spoke
through it. The Bible itself had only a secondary and dependent
authority. It was the channel, the medium, the occasion of God's
Word: it could not be identified with God's Word itself. Hence
Luther regarded parts of the Bible with a very critical spirit. The
Epistle of James with its stress on "works" he considered an
epistle of "straw."

This Word of God awakens and creates in man faith, the
assurance of God's forgiveness, trust in Christ. Faith is not belief

in a proposition; it is not assent to a statement of fact. It is a matter of spiritual life or death, and concerns man's ultimate salvation. It is decision about things eternal: it deals with man's final destiny, the ultimate meaning of his life. It is trust, confidence, assurance that God has forgiven man through Christ. Faith is a thing of power: it overwhelms. It assures man of pardon and excites in him loving service. It is at once the gift of God and man's response to God. By it is the Church created.

One of Luther's favourite expressions for the Church is *Sanctorum Communio*. He gave the phrase a new meaning. He interpreted it not as "fellowship with the saints," but as "the community of the saints." The Church was a community of people, bound together by this faith. It was not an institution which mediated God's grace. It did not stand between man and God. It was the company of God, His people, the gathering of those who had heard the Word, and who trusted in Christ. By calling Christians saints Luther did not mean that they were morally perfect, but that they were called to be perfect. The holiness of the Church was neither the moral holiness that comes from man's own striving, nor was it the sacramental holiness, which Luther caricatured when he wrote, "Just throw a surplice over your head and you are holy with the Roman Church's holiness." Rather did Luther regard the true sanctity of the Church as that purity of life which was created in man by the dynamic and powerful Word of God. Its virtues are simple. They excluded wrath, hatred, envy, and vengeance. They sprang simply from the heart for God's sake. They were not the actions of men striving to win merit; they were the spontaneous expression of those who were recreated by the power of God in Christ.

This community extended all over the world; it embraced the ages; it was measured by no thought or institution of man. It was God's own creation, and it was known only by faith. Belief in the Church, to Luther, was an article of faith.[1] No one could see with the eye of sense who was holy or who was a true believer. These things transcended human sight, but for that very reason they were most real. The Church was no figment of the imagination.

In his doctrine of the Church Luther referred to an "inner" and an "outer" Christendom. By the former he meant the essential, real and true Church—the Christian assembly of one accord in faith the world over. That is the soul of the Church, its inner life and meaning. By outer Christendom he signified the external manifestation of that Christian community, its exterior organisation, the visible local congregations with their rites and buildings and ministry. These he called the "body" of the Church, which was vitalised by the "soul" and had no meaning or life apart from the soul.

Thus in Luther there are not two Churches, there are not two distinct entities, visible and invisible Church. Rather does he think in terms of the organic unity of the real Church with its outward manifestation, though he will not confuse or identify these two aspects of the single reality. He makes it clear that all the visible and external signs of the Church, its sacraments and its ministry, can exist without faith, and hence are not necessarily an indication of the true Church. Yet he is equally insistent that the people of God, who have faith, express their life in a religious community which is marked by the sacraments, the ministry,

---

[1]Calvin likewise held that belief in the Church was an article of faith, but he attempted to make the distinction, which he supported from Augustine and other Latin fathers, between belief in God or Christ as *personal objects* of faith, and belief in the resurrection or the visible and invisible Church as *articles* of faith. He cited the distinction in the Latin creed between *Credo in Deum* and *Credo sanctam ecclesiam,* which philologically is unsound, since the Greek text has a preposition in both places.

and above all by the preaching of the Word. Faith and community in Luther are inseparably united. He is often at pains to stress that this community or Christendom shares a common life. "No one calls anything his own"; each is helped by the prayers and Christian life of other believers. They are mutually supported and strengthened, bearing one another's burdens.

When he comes to consider the place of the ministry in this Christian community, Luther rejects altogether the claim of the Roman Church to mediate by its priesthood between God and the people. He holds that all Christians are priests: all can approach God through the one Mediator, Jesus Christ. The ministers are but the public administrants of that which essentially belongs to the congregation. For convenience and order it is impossible for all to baptise, consecrate the sacrament, or preach. The ministry is appointed by the community to act for them. The people of God commit to chosen representatives the exercise of rights that really belong to every faithful Christian.

Both the strength and the weakness of Luther's position derive from his conviction that the Christian community is the spontaneous creation of faith. With deep insight he saw that the assurance of God's mercy is a continual Christian experience, and expresses itself in the communal life of Christian worship and in the ordinary relationships of Christians in the world. He was convinced that the normal vocations of life could have a Christian character. Man did not need to shut himself up in a monastery and adopt a rule of self-discipline in order to gain high favour with God. Rather did every pursuit of life provide occasion for Christian service. No matter what a man's social status was, he could express the power of his faith in obedience to God's commandments and in humbly performing the duties of life which his occupation laid upon him. Out of this very insight grew the

weakness of Luther's position. He believed that these social distinctions and the political powers, upon which they were based,
had a divine foundation, and everything verging on social or
political revolution was contrary to the command of God. Only
on one occasion did he overthrow this conviction. At a critical
moment in the fortunes of the Protestant cause, he contended
that the territorial German princes had a right to war against the
Emperor when he tried to enforce upon them the Roman Catholic
religion. Luther attempted to justify his position by claiming
God had intended that Germany should be ruled by the princes
and not by the Emperor. He further claimed that men had a right
to defend themselves against a false religion. Apart from this
instance, Luther never advanced a criterion by which to judge
the relatively unjust social and political relations of the world,
and by which to strive for a society more in conformity with the
will of God. With deep Christian conviction he believed that
all the deeds and institutions of men stood condemned by the
Holy Judgment of God; but he seemed to think that the only
possible way for some kind of rough justice to be accomplished
in the world was for the prince to take his task seriously and to
try to act in the best interests of his people. Such ideal princes
were hard to find and Luther himself indulged in the remark,
that princes were most often the greatest fools or the worst knaves
on earth. Nevertheless, in one of his treatises he did try to outline the conduct of the Christian prince, and his advice is characterised for the most part by a shrewd and practical judgment.

By overthrowing all idea of the Church as an institution, which
could guard and to some extent enforce the law of justice in the
world, Luther left his faith at the mercy of the secular powers.
In a variety of ways they actually controlled the religious situation
in such territories as Saxony and Hesse. Luther clearly saw that

the claim of the Roman Church to be God's representative on earth was as false as it was presumptuous. The Christian community must cast the searchlight of God's judgment upon all the proud and corrupt justice of men. But Luther did not grasp that the Church is also committed to discovering means to enforce that rough justice, which makes for social and political improvement in the world. It is true that the alliance of Protestantism with the secular princes was the only practical way of establishing the Evangelical Church in Germany and of defeating the Roman Catholic powers. Yet that alliance was made fatally dangerous to the prophetic vitality of the Church. Its members tried to live a life of personal Christian piety in their various vocations, but, in their corporate unity as Christians, they were not directly concerned with the justice and government of the world. So it was that the Evangelical Church in Germany became an example *par excellence* of the territorial church system, against which the papacy had struggled since the days of Charlemagne and the Saxon Emperors. The interests of the Church became uniquely allied with those of the local territories. The final religious and political relationship, which the long wars between the Roman Catholic and Protestant powers in Germany produced, was one in which the local prince determined the religious destiny of his territory—*cuius regio, eius religio* (1555).

CALVIN

The development of Protestantism in Geneva followed a somewhat different course from that in Germany. Geneva lay on the great trade route of Europe and was growing to be a commercial centre of importance. The cause of the Reformation was linked with the interests of the middle classes, who had successfully thrown off the yoke of the ducal House of Savoy along with the Roman Catholic religion. The rise of capitalism, as an economic and social system to displace the ancient feudal basis of society, had made rapid strides in such trading centres. It had brought with it a sense of individualism and independence, which replaced the consciousness of organic unity and mutual obligation, characteristic of the Middle Ages. The religious development of Protestantism in Geneva reflected these circumstances to a far greater degree than did the course of the early Reformation in Germany, where capitalism had made headway only in cities like Augsburg. Luther's outlook was thoroughly agrarian. He thought in terms of the simple relationships of life, of the farm and of the small village. The organic unity of life with its diverse social stations and their mutual interdependence is reflected no less in his idea of vocation than in his idea of the church as the Christian community. The more complicated relationships of life, finance, capital, interest, he regards as basically evil and to be avoided. His constant plea is for the simplicity of German life, free from Italian intervention and from the corrupting influences of the great financial families, like the Fuggers, who were the papal bankers.

With Geneva it was different. Calvin was forced to come to grips with an expanding capitalistic system. In common with the later scholastics, who had seen that the papal finances depended upon this new system, he was willing to allow the legitimacy of taking interest on loans, a practice which had formerly been banned as unchristian. The typical ideal for the Christian life became the successful business man, careful, shrewd, and industrious. The ascetic principle, formerly applied only to the monasteries, was now preached as the self-discipline required by God in the normal vocations of life. Luxury and sloth were to be banished by diligence and frugal living. Success in this life was regarded as the providential reward of hard work. In later Puritan ethics this hardheaded business Christianity led to a fatal identification of success with virtue and of poverty with sloth. Men failed to have the slightest understanding of capitalism and its tragic effects upon labor and prices. Nevertheless, it must be admitted that Calvin's legislation in Geneva to regulate prices and hinder monopolies was aimed directly to prevent the corruptions and evils that he saw were inherent in the system.

Calvin was at one with the democratic spirit which this new capitalism had advanced. Money was power, and it could effectively challenge the ancient feudal authority of the long-established families. The rulers of Geneva became the rich middle classes. Though they liked to style themselves "the people" and talk in an ingratiating way about democracy, they really represented a limited class in the Genevan population and controlled the government with a firm hand. Yet in his political theory Calvin showed a more liberal spirit than Luther. Though he deplored anything that verged on popular revolution, he maintained that the people should have true representatives to guard and protect their interests and to overthrow from office rulers who became tyrants. In the Church he advocated the popular election of the ministers, though in Geneva they were generally appointed with the mutual consent of the clergy and the civic council.

The differences between Luther and Calvin lie deeper than in the contrast of their diverse backgrounds. Calvin was the organising genius of the Reformation: Luther was its prophetic spirit. Calvin brought to the Protestant cause exactly what it had so far lacked—discipline and order. As a lawyer and a Frenchman he was well fitted to play the part to which he was called. He had a lucid grasp of law and order and a shrewd and calculating judgment, which made him an excellent administrator. He saved

the Reformation from the chaos into which the prophetic spirit
alone might have reduced it. He made the Genevan Church an
institution which became the centre of the Protestant cause in
Europe. In its rights and organisation the Church was clearly
distinct from the secular authority and, within limits, exerted over
it a certain religious control. Geneva was committed to the Reformed religion, which was enforced by the State as the supporter
and protector of the Church. Such a relationship involved the
same problem which had agitated the Middle Ages. Which was
the final authority, the Church or the secular power (organised
in a number of councils)? Calvin struggled to preserve for the
Church an independence from secular control, though he was
hindered in this by the fact that the councils had the ultimate
material power. However, though Calvin's struggle to ensure the
Church's freedom continued long, and for a time caused his
banishment from Geneva, it did finally issue in a relative independence for the Church. Under Calvin, Geneva became something of a theocratic city-state. As a haven for Protestant refugees,
it was the centre of the Reformed cause in Europe. The influence
of Geneva spread to France, England, Scotland,[2] and the Netherlands. Reformers, who had been disciplined in the thought and
churchly practice of Calvin, carried abroad the spirit of Puritanism
and democracy, which was so vitally to affect the fortunes of
Europe and America.

The controlling thought in Calvin about the nature of the
Church is summed up in his distinction of the Church invisible

[2]Aside from the *Institutes of the Christian Religion*, the basic ideas of Calvinism
are to be found in the *Westminster Confession*, the authoritative standard of doctrine in the Presbyterian Church. This confession was adopted by the General Assembly of Scotland in 1647, displacing the former confession which had largely
been the work of John Knox. In America the General Synod of the Presbyterian
Church approved it in 1729, and some necessary amendments have been made
since 1788.

and visible. The former was the unknown body of God's elect, whom he had chosen for salvation. Calvin did not think of this number of the predestined in purely individualistic terms. He had a real sense of the corporate body of true Christians, knit together in a transcendent unity, and sharing a common spiritual life as members of Christ and heirs of the blessings of God.[3] Together they formed a fellowship, in which the various members communicated their gifts and graces to one another and participated in the vital spiritual life, which was found in obedience to Christ. Especially in corporate Christian worship was this awareness of the Church as a fellowship of common faith and life made real. It was a unity that reached out beyond the world and the ages, and one in which all true believers shared. But Calvin refused to identify this transcendent spiritual body with any temporal manifestation in history. It was something which only the eye of faith could perceive.

Yet the Church, as it was organised in history, had great significance for him. It was the occasion of man's entering into that relationship with God, which made him a member of this spiritual fellowship. The Church visible was the ecclesiastical institution upon earth, distinguished by the preaching of the Word and the administration of the two sacraments of baptism and the Lord's

[3]This is the idea that lies behind the Protestant use of the term "Catholic." The Church is Catholic, because, as John Knox's Confession of Faith asserts, "it includes the elect of all ages, realmes, natiouns, and tongues." Furthermore, there is a qualitative as well as a quantitative sense in the use of the word. In its Protestant and original meaning of "universal," it refers not only to the aggregate number of all Christians, but to the transcendent unity and fellowship which exist between them. As Calvin clearly states it, "The Church is called Catholic or universal; because there could not be two or three churches, without Christ being divided, which is impossible. But all the elect of God are so connected with each other in Christ, that as they depend upon one head, so they grow up together as into one body, compacted together like members of the same body; being made truly one, as living by one faith, hope, and charity, through the same Divine Spirit, being called not only to the same inheritance of eternal life, but also to a participation of one God and Christ."

Supper. Calvin really reproduced much of the theory of Augustine. His marks of the Church as an institution were certainly fewer and different, and the claims he made for it were less extreme. Nevertheless, the basic distinction between the visible and invisible Church was Augustinian in idea.

The relationship which Calvin attempted to establish between these two ideas of the Church was one of discipline. To belong to the visible Church was the command of God. Although He might have saved man in some other way, the way He has chosen and revealed is one which demands his obedience and submission to the institution of the Church. The idea of discipline as a mark of the Church played a very significant rôle in Puritan thinking, which had its roots in John Calvin. The chief value of the Church as an institution was that it trained the elect, not only acquainting them with the knowledge of salvation but guiding and ruling them in every detail of the religious and moral life. It is not an exaggeration to say that the seriousness of the Reformers in Geneva made for an ecclesiastical intolerance and close moral supervision, which surpassed that of the medieval Church.

The Church in Geneva was strict and rigid in its demands upon its members. Its close contact with the secular authority made the religious and moral supervision of the citizens of Geneva a matter of civic concern. Calvin held the same thesis as Augustine, that the State should act as a pious father to its citizens. It should support the true worship of God and defend the constitution of the Church. All citizens were regarded as Church members and came under the discipline of its authorities. Twelve lay elders, appointed annually from the various city councils, paid visits to all the families in Geneva, and saw that their doctrine was orthodox and their conduct beyond reproach. Whenever they discovered serious sins, the offenders were brought up for trial before the consistory—a kind of ecclesiastical court made up of clerical and lay members. If they were found guilty and deserving of punishment, they were handed over to the State for appropriate chastisement. Accounts of several cases have come down to us. For instance, a term of three days' imprisonment was visited upon some irreligious scoffers caught laughing during the sermon on a Sunday morning. A man was banished from the city for three months for remarking, when he heard an ass bray, "He chants a fine Psalm!" A girl was beheaded for striking her parents, and a banker of some prominence was executed for adultery. Compulsory attendance at worship was demanded and a fine of three sols was exacted from those who failed to be present.

Most of these laws go back to the police regulations of medieval towns, where the most minute details were laid down for the conduct of life. Dress appropriate to one's social station, the number of dishes to be served at meals, the number of dances proper for festal occasions were the subjects of strict legislation. However, it was the legalistic spirit of Calvinism which revived such regulations and gave them an added strictness. The religious emphasis was everywhere reflected and laws against blasphemy were particularly severe. A man who was heard swearing by the body and blood of Christ was once pilloried for an hour. The moral tone of Geneva was admittedly low when Calvin came, and its general disorder was not a little due to the fervid but unpractical preaching of his Protestant predecessors like Farel. A passion to destroy the Roman Churches and their images was more characteristic of Geneva than the strict sobriety of the good life. This helps us to explain something of Calvin's insistence upon discipline.

Severity was meted out equally to both sexes and to families of obscure and of distinguished origin. Geneva was to be a model state, disciplined in its religious and moral life, a pattern of Puritan seriousness for the whole of Europe.

The Church itself claimed no right to inflict civil punishments. The final discipline it could impose was that of excommunication. All it could do in other cases was to hand the offender over to be punished by the State. In the matter of excommunication, however, Calvin claimed that the Church should be free from secular control. At first the Council refused to admit this independent right, and Calvin had to struggle long before he could gain his point. Finally he succeeded, although the struggle cost him a temporary banishment from Geneva. Beneath the issue lay the old problem of the medieval conflict between Pope and Emperor, and while the Church enjoyed some independence during the lifetime of Calvin, as soon as his influence was gone secular control was largely reasserted. The State had the final power with the force of arms. Unlike the papacy, the Protestants had neither the independent territory of the States of the Church nor the spiritual armies of the monks to aid them in their struggle against secular domination.

CALVIN AND SERVETUS

The most dramatic scandal that attaches to the Reformation is the burning of Servetus in 1553. As this raises two of the fundamental questions of the Reformation, the relation of Church and State, and the problem of ultimate authority, it may not be inappropriate to recount the story.

The two contestants in this struggle had much in common. They were both in the prime of life. Calvin was by two years the senior of Servetus, who suffered death at the age of forty-two. Both had been precocious youths and had early evidenced keen genius and independent thinking. Calvin produced the first edition of his immortal *Institutes* at the age of twenty-six, while Servetus had written his first incisive attack upon the doctrine of the Trinity when he was barely twenty years old.

There their similarities end. Servetus was a Spaniard, quick-tempered and given at times to fiery denunciation. He was a man of vast learning, whose checkered career had made him a master of many subjects. He had lectured in Paris on geometry and astronomy, studied medicine, and published a distinguished work on syrups. He had even practiced as a physician in Vienne. In all his activity he gave evidence of his strong individuality, and frequently incurred the censure of those who upheld orthodox opinions whether in science or in theology. In personal appearance he was slender and delicate with a high forehead and flowing beard.

Calvin, on the other hand, was essentially the Frenchman. He was sharp-featured with a pointed black beard and with a complexion pallid and dark, but with eyes whose clear lustre reflected something of the acumen of his genius. He was a man of indomitable will and purpose who in thought no less than in action pursued a given course with relentless insistency and logic. He had not the wide range of knowledge or the broad sympathy of Servetus, but he was his superior in theological learning and in lucidity and accuracy.

Calvin had probably come into contact with Servetus in Paris. There the latter was studying mathematics and physics under the assumed name of Villeneuve, fearing to reveal his identity, lest the Roman Inquisition should detect him as the author of the attack on the Trinity. Later on, however, after Calvin had left for Geneva, the two men carried on a lengthy correspondence on theological issues. In the course of this, Servetus clearly re-

vealed his unorthodox opinions on the Trinity, and even outlined
a sectarian view of the Church as a spiritual kingdom, whose
ultimate authority was the living voice of the Spirit. This was a
position which must have seemed wildly subjective to Calvin
with his genius for organisation. To him the Church was distinguished by the preaching of the word and by the two sacraments,
while the final authority was Holy Scripture, somewhat legalis-
tically interpreted.

Calvin replied to these views of Servetus with outspoken denunciation and he even told Farel that if the heretic came to
Geneva, "I shall never suffer him to depart alive." It is true that
this interchange of letters had exasperated Calvin. His opponent
wrote in a somewhat disputatious spirit and assumed an air of
presumption and arrogance. In his basic attack upon the doctrine
of the Trinity, Servetus revealed great erudition and a fine power
of argument, but these very qualities only made his case worse
in Calvin's eyes. The main thesis of Servetus was that the doctrine
of three persons in one God was an example of the metaphysical
sophism of Greek theology, which had led Christianity away
from its original meaning and purity. He refused to regard Jesus
Christ as the Eternal Son of God, styling Him rather the Son of
the Eternal God. He claimed He did not exist as a person prior
to the incarnation. Rather was He an idea in the mind of the
Father, potentially, not actually present. To Servetus the orthodox
doctrine of the Trinity was a "philosophic pest," which involved
Tritheism. To obviate the difficulty he revived, in a somewhat
original way, the teaching of Sabellius, contending that creation,
redemption and the activity of the Holy Spirit were three manifestations of God, which did not imply distinctions in the God-
head. In his anxiety to emphasise the unity of the Deity he
developed a type of pantheism, regarding God as a pervading

essence of which all things are manifestations. But for all his attack on the traditional doctrine, Servetus had no intention of detracting from Christ. Around Him he centered his passionate religious piety, referring to Him as "my unique Master," and even going so far as to say that without Him we could have no knowledge of God at all.

The ideas of Servetus found classic expression in his major work, *The Restitution of Christianity,* in which he claimed that the Reformers no less than the Catholics had departed from the true, original faith and had corrupted Christianity, which he had been called to restore again to its pure form. He published the work anonymously (under the initials M. S. V.), and it was only indirectly and through his correspondence with Calvin that its authorship was finally revealed to the Roman Church.

One of Calvin's friends in Geneva had made reference to Servetus in a letter to a cousin, Arneys of Lyons. This letter Arneys, who was a Roman Catholic, promptly handed over to the Inquisition. He was only able to make good the accusation against Servetus by getting from Calvin the former correspondence, where Servetus had outlined his views and had even sent him part of the manuscript of the *Restitution.* It must be admitted that Calvin handed the letters over with some reluctance, but he cannot be regarded as altogether blameless of taking opportunity of this occasion to get the heretic condemned.

At the trial in Vienne Servetus (still under his assumed name of Villeneuve) prevaricated about his opinions, disclaiming he held them. He had only written them to Calvin as a kind of exercise to see what he would say in answer to them. He denied he was the author of his original work against the Trinity, although he had asserted it in one of the letters. Furthermore, he contended he had merely impersonated Servetus, the true author, for the sake of theological debate. Finally, he offered to submit in all things to the judgment of the Roman Church. After this examination good fortune temporarily favoured him and he effected an escape from prison, intending to seek refuge and seclusion in Italy. On his way he foolishly went to Geneva and, wishing to hear Calvin preach, attended church on Sunday. He was recognised and immediately arrested on the instigation of Calvin. At once he was put on trial for heresy and a number of articles were drawn up against him, including charges of defaming Calvin and holding opinions contrary to Holy Scripture. The trial lasted from August 14 to October 26 and was a bitter contest, not only between Calvin and Servetus, but between Calvin and his opponents in Geneva.

The full significance of the condemnation of Servetus can be grasped only when it is remembered that Calvin was then engaged in a major conflict for power in Geneva. The independence of the Church from the secular authority was at stake, and Servetus made some capital out of the uncertain position of Calvin. He was defended by men like Perrin, who led the opposition in defying the ecclesiastical power of the Consistory. During the trial of Servetus the important case of Philibert Berthelier came up. He was a man of admittedly loose and disorderly life and the preceding year had been excommunicated by the Consistory. When, however, the anti-Calvinistic party gained a majority in the elections of 1533, he appealed to the Council and with the aid of his powerful friends was able to get the order of excommunication reversed. The Council gave him a document of acquittal, thus assuming the right of excommunication which Calvin claimed belonged exclusively to the Consistory. Calvin thus found himself in an awkward predicament. To refuse to recognise the Council's decision was to make himself a political rebel: to allow it was to renounce his whole position. Happily for him the storm blew over. He preached an ardent sermon on that communion Sunday, forbidding all those who were unworthy to partake of the sacrament. To keep peace Berthelier's powerful friends advised him to stay away. Calvin's triumph in Geneva was not assured until the following year when his opponents were routed in the 1554 elections. This precipitated a street riot of grave proportions and gave him the opportunity to rid himself of his former enemies. Several of the leaders, like Perrin and Berthelier, saved themselves from arrest by flight, while others were either condemned to death or banished.

But to return to the trial of Servetus. Halfway through the prosecution the Roman Inquisition in Vienne sent word that the heretic, being a fugitive from justice, should be returned to them. The choice of trial by Protestants or Catholics was given to Servetus and he decided for the former, imploring his Protestant captors not to send him back to Vienne. Though his protest was granted it finally availed him nothing, for Calvin pursued his enemy to death with no less bitterness and determination than the Romanists.

The final stage of the conflict was reached when Servetus was commanded to put his theological opinions in writing, in reply to a series of articles drawn up by Calvin. These the Reformer drew up with his accustomed skill and they were so worded as to bring out the errors of his opponent. The replies of Servetus clearly showed his variance with orthodox doctrine, and were duly condemned by the other Swiss churches to whom appeal was also made. The case of Servetus was even further aggravated by the unmeasured and reckless terms in which he attacked Calvin in these replies. He had sealed his doom, and was finally condemned by the Council to be burned at the stake, October 27,

1553. He died crying, "Jesus, Son of the Eternal God, have mercy upon me."

Calvin had won, and he had vindicated his position in two particulars. He had successfully defeated the opposition, who even to the last pleaded for a more favourable verdict on the accused, and he had also asserted his interpretation of the Holy Scriptures as the final authority of the Genevan Reformation. This latter issue came more clearly to the fore a year later in the condemnation of another of Calvin's opponents, Castellion. He denied the canonicity of the Song of Solomon, and managed to escape any such tragic fate as that of Servetus by quitting Geneva at the right moment. Nevertheless, the same question was involved as in the defeat of Servetus. The opinions of Calvin triumphed, and his particular interpretation of Holy Scripture became the final authority. For instance, during the prosecution, Servetus had claimed that Isaiah 53 referred historically to Cyrus and not to Christ, a contention stoutly denied by Calvin. In a similar way Servetus had questioned the truth of the statement that Palestine was literally a land flowing with milk and honey—something that seemed to him a geographical absurdity. Such free thinking Calvin regarded as blasphemy: it was virtually accusing Moses of being a liar. In the light of this we can well appreciate the statement of Richard Hooker, "The sense of Scripture which Calvin alloweth," is of more weight than if "ten thousand Augustines, Jeromes, Chrysostoms, Cyprians, or whoever else were brought forth." Calvin's legalistic mind, fruitful as it was in producing the powerful Genevan Church, the centre of European Protestantism, was none the less detrimental to the Reformed cause. He tended to regard Scripture as literally infallible. Unlike Luther, he did not view it as the occasion of God's Word to man. The same infallibility that the Roman Church had claimed was now attributed to the literal sense of Scripture. This became a stumbling-block for future generations and deprived the Reformation of some of its profoundest insights. It is not the literal words of the Bible, but God's Word to man, incarnate in Jesus Christ and spoken through the living Church, its faith, its tradition, its Scriptures, and its life, which is the only final authority for Christianity.[4]

Servetus had been tried and condemned by a secular court. He had written during the trial to the Council, denouncing this as an innovation contrary to Scripture and to the practice of the Apostles and the Early Church. Moreover, he claimed to be innocent of any crime done on Genevan soil and of any sedition. In itself this secular trial is not of very grave importance, for Calvin took a leading part in it and the Consistory would have condemned Servetus anyway. Furthermore, the final statements of Servetus, as we have seen, were submitted to the ecclesiastical authority of the other Swiss churches. What is of more importance is the question of the right of the secular power to condemn to death those whom the Church regards as heretics. How did Calvin justify himself? He wrote a defence the following year, in which he claimed to be in possession of the infallible Word of God, and by this to be able to judge false doctrine which is apostasy from God. In the light of this it is the duty of the temporal power to eradicate everything that is subversive of true religion and which detracts from the honour of God. When more liberal spirits claimed Calvin was returning to the barbarities of the Roman Church, he answered that the essential point was not that persecution was wrong, but that the grounds on which

---

[4]The *Westminster Confession* states this succinctly, "God alone is lord of the conscience, and hath left it free from the doctrines and commandments of men which are in any thing contrary to his Word, or beside it, in matters of faith or worship."

the Roman Church persecuted were false. They were blasphemers and the children of darkness: he was the upholder of the honour of God.

While it would be quite erroneous to regard Calvin as a Torquemada, who in eighteen years of office executed perhaps some 8,800 victims, his basic theory of persecution was the same. He claimed an absolute authority for those particular doctrines and theological interpretations which he upheld, and he believed that heresy was so dangerous to the life of the Christian state that it merited the death penalty.

Religious persecution is of all forms the most blasphemous, because it claims to act in the name of God and elevates human decisions and judgments to the sphere of the divine. One thing that the liberal era, which emerged out of the bitter European wars of religion, has taught us, is that these judgments are relative and human and cannot claim any universal and divine authority. Toleration, while it has often come to mean indifference to religious opinions, should mean humility, and a recognition that man cannot presume to be God.

HOOKER

The English Reformation was in many ways unique. Its development was gradual. It did not represent so clear a break with the past as did the movements under Luther and Calvin. It was characteristically English in its desire to preserve what was best in the past tradition and to emphasise the continuity of the Church through the ages. It laid more stress upon the practical life and organisation of the Church than upon doctrine. Indeed, the Reformation in England was heralded by no strong prophetic voice like Luther's and produced no great theologian of the calibre of Calvin.

One of the main factors in the background of the English development was a strong national consciousness and a hatred of foreign encroachments. Henry VIII, whose unfortunate marriages precipitated the break with Rome, had united in his person the houses of York and Lancaster, whose feudal rivalries had long wasted England in the civil wars of the Roses. Henry's policy was one of creating a highly centralised government to subdue the power of the feudal barons. He ruled with absolutism, and achieved some measure of success in forming England into a self-conscious and self-sufficient national power. English patriotism found its centre of unity in this despotic monarch, whose cruel and avaricious nature was not without some redeeming characteristics, among which was his genius for ruling men. There is certainly a dark side to his reign. He debased the coinage, destroyed the art of the monasteries, and hindered, far more than advanced, letters and scholarships. He beheaded More and Fisher, executed Surrey, and put Wyatt in prison. Yet if he ruled as a tyrant he did not fail in creating a highly centralised power and in fostering a spirit of patriotism. Thus he laid the foundations of the splendid Elizabethan era.

Under Henry the religious situation was Catholic in general thought and feeling, but national in organisation. The doctrines of Protestantism made little advance till the succeeding reign of Edward VI, when the Calvinistic influence came to be felt. Yet the way was prepared for a thorough Reformation when Henry transferred to the kingship the ecclesiastical power which had previously been centred in the papacy. His break with Rome, the immediate cause of which was doubtless to gratify his lust, was one more example of his national and centralising policy. He destroyed the monasteries with ruthless cruelty, because they were the centres of the papal power in England. He parcelled out their lands to newly ennobled families, in order to make dependent upon him a body of wealth and privilege, which would be an effective check against the ancient feudal nobles. Henry's policy gave to the English Church the stamp it was to bear till the present day. It was to be national, centred as far as its temporal organisation was concerned in the kingship. Furthermore, the very fact that this reorganisation took place with little change in the doctrine and theology of the old Catholicism, marked the English development with a certain conservatism in religious feeling, which it never lost. During the reigns of Edward VI and Elizabeth, Catholic and Protestant elements were finally combined in a religion essentially practical, and with a fine taste for tradition and continuity. There was, moreover, in the English temperament a hatred of over-simplification and a genius for forming institutions. These elements were reflected in the growth of the English Church. Though it was marked by doctrinal inconsistencies and theological temporising, it had about it an institutional excellence.

The most typical example of English religious thought was Richard Hooker (d. 1600), whose *Laws of Ecclesiastical Polity* was the first Reformed English writing to arouse the admiration of the Roman Church. Written in superb literary style, it comprehends both Catholic and Protestant elements, and is an attempt to examine the nature and polity of the Church as an institution. It is written from a definitely practical point of view and, although it reflects deep theological thinking, it is directed to questions of immediate moment for the English Church. The work is typically English. It is marked by sane and moderate judgment, by a love of tradition and liberty, and is well described by the word "judicious."

Hooker begins his book by an examination of the nature of

law and of those principles which are necessary for the formation of ordinary societies in the world. In one sense the Church is such an ordinary or natural society, having as its origin the common inclination of all men to social life. Yet the Church is something more than this. It is supernatural, because it is bound together and governed by a law that God has revealed, and by a type of worship and relationship toward Him which is not the product of man's natural reason and capacity. God, in His goodness, has made possible for man a bond of association with Him and with his fellows, which brings salvation from sin and death.

What is this Church of which Hooker speaks? How can it be known? Like Calvin, Hooker here distinguishes between the true Church, the transcendent body of those who are really members of the Church mystical (he prefers this term to "invisible"), and those visible, apparent societies on earth which claim to be the Church. No one can tell by the eye of sense who belongs to the mystical body, for that is something to be discerned by faith, and its full number is known only to God. Yet, when we talk of the Church in the world, we mean definite and visible societies, to which it is the duty of Christians to belong for common worship and for corporate life in the faith. These visible communions are really one, bound together by their common allegiance to Christ and by their participation in the sacraments. However, for the sake of convenience, they are organised in different localities and need not share the same type of polity. There may be many who attach themselves to these societies, but by their impiety and wickedness they are not members of the Church mystical. This, however, does not vitiate the purpose and nature of these Christian communions. To some extent they share the common life in Jesus Christ. Some may be sounder than others, some more corrupt, but their allegiance to one Lord, one faith, and one baptism give them their essential Christian significance.

A somewhat more Catholic aspect of Hooker's thought on the Church appears when he considers the Incarnation. In common with early Christianity, Hooker regards the Incarnation as the relating of divinity to humanity. Man is endued with the "supernatural gifts, graces, and effects" of divinity, through the coming of Christ and by faith in Him. This relationship to God is realised by man's adoption into the Church, the visible society which has Christ as its head and is made one body by its mystical conjunction with Him. Especially is this union of the Church with God manifested in the Eucharist, which God has commanded as an instrument whereby He makes available for man His abounding grace. Unlike the medieval scholastics, Hooker does not conceive of the elements themselves as miraculously changed into the body and blood of Christ. Rather does he take the view of the Early Church. Through the sacramental act and along with it, God gives His divine power to the true believer.

When he considers the polity appropriate for the Church, Hooker finds himself in keen opposition to the Puritans. Calvin's legalistic mind had led him to advocate the Presbyterian system as the only one ordained by God and described in the New Testament. It was really among the Puritans, and not among the Anglicans, that the idea of a single, divinely prescribed form of Church government first originated. Under the Presbyterian system the terms bishop and presbyter were regarded as synonymous, and all ministers were looked upon as equals. In theory they were to be elected by the local community and to fulfil the functions of preaching, leading worship, and pastoral care. They were to be assisted by lay elders in the administration of discipline.

The ordination of the ministers, by the laying on of hands by other pastors, signified that their authority had a divine source. Their democratic election and the firm conviction shared by all the Reformers, that every true believer was a priest and had direct access to God through Christ, guarded against the sacerdotal tendency of the Roman Church. Hooker opposed this theory on several grounds. He claimed that no single type of polity was prescribed in Holy Scripture. Moreover, since inequality was of the nature of all government, it was neither necessary nor convenient for ministers to have equal rank. He contended that the traditional orders of bishop, presbyter, and deacon, which had the sanction of a long tradition, should be kept. He stressed the fact that the ministry derived its authority from God and not from the laity, although the latter had some part in their election.[5] This led him to oppose the Calvinistic system of lay elders, which he regarded as lay interference in the Church. The Church, he claimed, must be administered only by those who have a divine authority. Like Calvin, he distinguished between two types of ministry, the ordinary and the prophetic. They were both from God, but the former were appointed by the Church, the latter were raised up by God for special purposes.

Hooker regards the bishops as the representatives of the Apostles, whom he claims were the bishops of the Early Church. While he is aware that the terms bishop and presbyter are sometimes used synonymously in the New Testament, he considers that the period of equal presbyters lasted only while the Apostles were there to control them. After that time the bishops received rights over the presbyters, which corresponded to the Apostolic

---

[5]In Hooker's theory the part that the laity had in canonical elections is represented by the royal appointments of bishops. The King is regarded as the constitutional representative of the people.

authority. Thus bishops, as the successors of the Apostles, had a power of government over presbyters as well as over the laity. Although some of Hooker's theory is not historically sound, he did clearly show that a uniform polity for the Church was neither inherent in Scripture nor in the nature of government. Furthermore, his insistence that the authority of the ministry is not derived from the people, but from God, reflects in his theory of government what the church has always maintained. Its gospel is of divine, and not of human, origin.

When Hooker deals with the relation of the Church to the State his theory well represents the concept of the national Church. He conceives that the purpose of government is not to provide a means of life but a means for living well. It has an ultimate religious destiny. The body politic is concerned with religion no less than with temporal affairs. There is a basic identity, not a fundamental difference, between Church and State. Every member of the commonwealth he considers to be a member of the Church of England, and the final end of natural society is one in which the temporal and the spiritual are knit together in unity.

Here Hooker clearly takes issue with the Roman Catholics and with the Puritans. Both these parties held that the Church must preserve its independence of the secular power: Hooker, on the other hand, claimed that the government of the Church and of the State were finally identical with political sovereignty. The King was supreme in both spheres of government, although he had no rights as a minister of the Church. Hooker looked back to the Hebrew people as his model of government. They were united, he remarked, "under one chief governor, on whose supreme authority did everything depend."

In this way he defends the King as the temporal ruler of the Church, but he clearly distinguishes between government and tyranny. The King must abide by law, and it is the function of the Parliament and of the Convocation respectively to interpret and represent the traditional law and custom of the two realms of Church and State. He has a contract theory of government. He holds that the authority of the King derives from the original agreement of the people, in which the King bound himself to rule by law and not by despotism. Hence, theoretically, he cannot override the decisions of Parliament or Convocation, and is limited by the law and tradition of the realm.

Hooker thus gave the national idealism of Tudor England a theory of Church and State, both broad and fitting the occasion. It presupposed a fundamental Christian culture which from the point of view of government was summed up in the political and religious duty of the kingship. Yet, inherent in this solution, was the gravest danger to the Church. It fell an easy prey to secular control, and for a long period (1717 to 1852) Convocation was forbidden to meet to consider ecclesiastical questions. Indeed, in the Elizabethan settlement, its powers had been disregarded and many of the religious acts which became law in the sixteenth century were never referred to Convocation. The Church thus came to be regarded as a department of the state and its ministers as political officials of religion. It lost its prophetic insight, which only its independence from the State could guarantee. With the almost complete secularisation of the State in the nineteenth century, the Church's position of dependence upon the political powers of King and Parliament became intolerable. This precipitated the Oxford Movement, whose champions looked to the divine foundation of the Church by

Christ as altogether independent of secular authority. It is an equally live issue today with the rejection by Parliament of the proposed revision of the Prayer Book in 1929.

Hooker's theory could have meaning only against the background of a Christian culture, which recognised the ultimate religious destiny of all political and social life. Even in those circumstances there was always a grave danger in the secular control of the Church. On the other hand, the close alliance of Church and State in England did not a little to temper politics with religious idealism. It gave English law and government something of the noble and impartial character for which it has been justly praised. Yet the danger of hypocrisy could not be escaped, for no national state can act absolutely in the interests of religion and at the same time guard its own power.

THE REFORMATION SECTS

The sectarian developments of the Reformation stand in marked contrast to those Protestant movements which came to terms with the social and political powers of the sixteenth century. The sects were either characterised by a desire to flee from the world and to live in the seclusion of godly piety, or else they were stirred by the vain hope that the Kingdom of God could be foreshadowed in some new political or social system.

The sectarian development, commonly known as Anabaptism, was a popular movement. It combined a variety of elements, social and religious. It derived much of its force from the social unrest of the early sixteenth century. It gave religious colour to the various peasant wars in Germany and in other parts of Europe. On its religious side it inherited many of those streams of thought which had come down from the late Middle Ages. The piety and moral earnestness of such movements as those of the "Brethren," were blended with the humanist spirit of the Renaissance. In short, the Anabaptists were the social radicals of their generation, but their radicalism was far from being purely secular. It had about it a religious fervour and true Christian devotion.

The Anabaptists can in no sense be regarded as a unified and cohesive movement. They formed little companies of devout believers scattered all over Germany and allied territories. Some of these were knit together in a loose kind of federation, but no such organisation had any permanent value. Among them could be found a vast variety of religious belief and practice. The number of their sects and their opinions, a contemporary writes, is impossible to know, and no two can be found to agree on all points. Some held millenarian views, others practised a real community of property, and others were characterised by their liberal charity. A good many of them maintained that infant baptism was a meaningless rite, and that entrance into the Church should be a matter of adult decision. It is from this view that they got the name Anabaptists. There were those among them who verged toward extreme religious mania. Tales have come down of women who uttered meaningless prophecies and of those who believed themselves to be Christ or even God. These, however, were the exceptions rather than the rule. By and large they were earnest religious folk of the underprivileged peasant classes. They allied themselves in spirit with the attack of the Reformers against the presumption and abuses of the Roman Church, but they regarded their constructive efforts with apprehension. With deep religious conviction they believed any true Reformation of the Church must involve the reform of social injustices, although they were divided on the question of the use of force to accomplish these ends.

Furthermore, they stood in clear opposition to the other Protestant parties in their view of the Church. Basic to their thought was the old Donatist conception. The Church was essentially a sect or a number of sects. They denied that it was an institution which had an intimate relation with the world and was organised and upheld by the secular power. Rather did they conceive of it as a number of small associations of believers who had fled from the world. By the purity of their personal life they witnessed to the fact that they renounced its evils, such as warfare, taking oaths in court, and holding political office. Most of them practised passive resistance and believed that the use of the sword was unconditionally forbidden by Christ. Others, of a more radical tendency, resorted to open rebellion to relieve peasant oppression and even "to bring in the Kingdom of God." In either case, the Church was interpreted as a small company of earnest believers who stood in marked contrast to the sin of the world. Either by passive resistance they renounced the world altogether, or else by the use of force they attempted to rectify its abuses and set up the true Kingdom of Christ on earth.

The social thinking of the Anabaptists was admittedly advanced and had great influence on the course of Christian history. Yet many dangers beset their idea of the nature of the Church. It ended either in complete separation from the world or else in fanatical absolutism, which attempted to build the Kingdom of God in history. The sect is an oversimplification of religious life. It does not fully grasp the problem that every religious and moral decision involves compromise, when it is put into actual practice. A further difficulty is that religion so easily becomes identified with morality and thus loses its deepest meaning and power. The sect type of religion fails to realise that all men's righteousness falls short of the glory of God, and yet at the same time in his repentance and contrition man is redeemed by God in Christ.

The story of the Münster Tragedy well illustrates one of the dangers inherent in every sectarian movement, which confuses deep religious conviction with political radicalism, instead of seeing their true relationship. What was attempted at Münster was to bring the Kingdom of God on earth. It was an example of religious and political tyranny, but it also exemplified an earnest desire to see social relationships in a religious light. Beside Luther's conviction that the peasant rising in Germany must be crushed with force of arms, the Münster experiment may appear almost enlightened. Luther, indeed, tried to justify his position, by claiming man was so fundamentally evil that God had provided constituted government to check his lawlessness and sin. But Luther did not clearly appreciate the fact that Christianity, while it does not immediately make men perfect, does lay upon them the obligation to decide for what is more just and relatively good in social and political relationships. The Anabaptists of Münster, on the other hand, went to the opposite extreme. They failed to recognise man's sin at all. They believed that they could set up or certainly foreshadow the perfect Kingdom, by bringing about the rule of God through the constitution of an actual theocratic state.

The abandonment of pacifism by the Anabaptists was largely due to the persecution they suffered at the hands of Roman Catholics and Protestants alike, and to the fervid preaching of those visionaries who imagined that the Kingdom of God was almost in sight. Among these was a baker, Jan Mathys, whose wild apocalyptic dreams had brought him many disciples. His lean figure and long black beard gave him something of the appearance of a prophet. He, with a tailor, Jan Bockelson, de-

cided that they would not wait for the Kingdom as other mil-
lennialists—notably Melchior Hoffman—had advised, but they
would inaugurate it themselves. The centre of their activity became Münster, where the Evangelical Lutheran doctrine had made
some headway by the third decade of the sixteenth century. The
townspeople, chafing under the rule of the bishop who was
also the secular prince of the city, had already raised several
insurrections and were easily won to the Reformation cause.
Furthermore, a humanist Reformer, Bernard Rothmann, with a
gift for popular preaching, had won the support and sympathy
of the poorer classes. Finally, the Lutherans gained the control
of the town council and ruled the city. But a new Anabaptist
element was coming to the fore, and Bernard Rothmann himself
was won over to their side. Refugees from the Anabaptist persecutions in other parts of Germany poured into Münster and
the city became the centre of millenarian hopes. With the aid
of the masses they gained control over the Lutheran element,
captured the town Council, and forced the prominent Lutherans
to leave the city. They demanded that all who remained should
be rebaptised.

Jan Mathys had become the most powerful figure in the city
and under him a communistic experiment was introduced. While
this may have had its origin in earlier Anabaptist teaching, some
very strict food regulations had become imperative, as the city
was being besieged by the combined armies of Roman Catholics
and Lutherans. The strict division of the food supply was an
attempt to save the city in the crisis. It is a strange contrast—
the wild hopes of the Anabaptists that the Kingdom was about
to appear, and the rigorous life of the city under siege!

The death of Jan Mathys, who seems to have walked out of
the city to purposeful martyrdom, was a severe blow to the

people. However, Jan Bockelson was elected king and with the abolition of the Council he ruled with twelve elders. Another stringent measure was then effected, which has caused severe criticism of these fanatics. A general order for polygamy was sent out. All men in the city were to take wives, and all women were to be under the care of a husband. No sexual irregularity was permitted and, although revolts were precipitated by the regulation, it was firmly enforced. To understand the law it is essential to realise that the city was overpopulated with women—some three to every man. Women had taken a leading part in the Anabaptist movement and had been instrumental in its success in Münster. They, too, were responsible for the suppression of the revolts against the law of polygamy. The large number of detached and unprotected women in the besieged city had doubtless been responsible for the promulgation of the law.

Jan Bockelson behaved as if he were the King of the New Israel and as if the millennium had started. When he rode through the city two boys walked before him, one carrying an Old Testament, and the other a sword, to symbolise the Divine Kingdom. All who met him fell on their knees in obeisance. One of his edicts begins, "The Kingdom long foreseen, promised by the mouth of the prophets, begun . . . by means of Christ and His Apostles, . . . and now come in John the Rightful, the promised and incontestable occupant of the Throne of David."

Such presumptuous notions only heralded the fall of Münster, which occurred in 1535, when the city was betrayed and the armies of the bishop broke through the defences. The citizens were massacred with ruthless cruelty, and the city streets were left covered with dead bodies and running with blood.

The tragedy of Münster lies in the attempt to give a final religious sanction to political idealism, and to imagine that man can usher in the Kingdom. Through the course of history religious-political radicalism has not seldom instanced such intolerance and fanaticism as characterised the government of Jan Bockelson. While we may deplore the lack of social vision on the part of those who persecuted the Anabaptists, we cannot neglect the fatal error in the idealism of the Münster Kingdom.

Related to the Anabaptist movement were the Baptists, who held to the same sectarian view of the Church and discarded infant baptism. After the ill-fated experiment in Münster, where some of the more extreme Anabaptists tried forcibly to set up the Kingdom of God on earth, they abandoned the policy of using force of arms. They were organised into peaceful and devout groups, whose serious and austere life contrasted with the general tenor of society around them. Under Menno Simons they were established in the Netherlands. From there they spread to England and to America, forming large bodies of dissent from the national and established churches. With champions like Roger Williams in Rhode Island the cause of religious liberty was advanced, and finally the complete separation of the Church from the State effected. At root this development presupposed the secularisation of the State, which was precipitated by the thinking of the Enlightenment.

The same conception of the Church as a number of small, voluntary associations of believers was upheld by the Independents or Congregationalists, who appeared in England in the late sixteenth century. They were the heirs of the Anabaptist movement, although they differed from the Baptists in retaining infant baptism. Nevertheless, they were firm in their contention that Church and State were independent and separate realms. The Church was composed of self-governing, separate communities of believers, and its organisation rested upon a covenant.

The members of the local congregation were united to God and to themselves by a free covenant, sealed by the rite of baptism. This idea was further extended to the secular sphere. In the *Mayflower* Compact the early Congregationalists, who emigrated to America, laid the foundation of American political theory, with the belief that government rests upon the free consent of the governed.

In England the Congregationalists stood in stern opposition to the national Church. To them the Church ought to be independent of all alliance with the secular government, because it was called out of the world to live the strict Christian life. They claimed that the Anglican discipline was too lax and the Church of England could not be called a true church, being, as John Robinson wrote, "clapped and clouted together of all persons of all sorts and spirits," and with a "pompous and imperious hierarchical government."

The most extreme form of this sectarian development was to be found in England in the seventeenth century with the Society of Friends (or Quakers), founded by George Fox (d. 1691). Their stress upon the inner light of the individual, as the only final authority in religion, led them to reject every regularised form of ministry. The only commission for preaching could be this direct, divine gift of immediate spiritual knowledge and insight. Those who preached were to depend only upon charity: they could claim no regular income. Freely they had received the word from God, freely they were to give it. Robert Barclay aptly described this view of the Church when he maintained it was "a company of such as God hath called out of the world and worldly spirit to walk in His light and life." Since God's light was made known in many ways that passed human understanding, the Church could have among its members, Jews,

Turks, and heathen and "all several sorts of Christians." The immediate knowledge of God by the inner light was the only authority in religion, and the only way by which man was joined to the Church of God. In their effort to purify religion of super-stition and to stress the importance of this real, inward devotion, the Quakers abandoned all sacraments and liturgical forms of prayer. Their worship was the worship of silence and of the freedom of the Spirit. There could be no distinction between clergy and laity, or male and female. All in the congregation were free to speak according as they were led by the spirit of God.

To the general tenor of social life around them they adopted an earnest and austere opposition. The commands of Christ they tried to obey with literal perfection. All flattery they rejected, refusing to sign letters with the hypocritical lie, "Your humble servant." In conversation they preferred the simple, "Thou" to the plural affectation, "You." They renounced all luxuries of food and apparel no less than all titles. They refused to take their hats off to any one, claiming that outward signs of adora-tion were reserved for God alone. To take oaths, swear, fight or actively to resist evil they refused as unchristian. Quakerism represents the most extreme position of individualism in religion. Yet none can deny their earnest and serious life and the great effect they have had upon Christianity by their uncompromising attitude toward war.

Sect and Church

The distinction between the "sect" and "church" idea of the religious community is roughly apparent in the antithesis that one is baptised as a child into a church, while association with a sect involves voluntary, adult decision. This difference, however, is seldom permanent, and the second generation of a sect often bears some of the marks characteristic of a church. An example of this can be seen in the adoption of the Half-Way Covenant by the New England Congregationalists in the seventeenth century. By this covenant even children of unregenerate parents, who had made no public confession of their faith, were accepted for baptism and granted partial membership in the religious community.

In general, however, it would be true to say that, by virtue of its voluntary membership and its opposition to the religious and ethical compromise of the church, the sect is characterised by moral earnestness and deep piety. In a variety of ways this has been expressed in the championing of the rights of the underprivileged, in renouncing war and kindred evils, and in stressing the purity of religious devotion. Through the course of Christian history the struggle between sect and church has frequently been the occasion of ethical reform and religious recovery.

The dangers in which the sect stands are those, on the one hand, of perfectionism and moralism; and on the other, of retreat from the world. In the former case the sectarian tends to confuse morality with religion, in the latter he ceases to have influence upon his world. While the sect avoids the peril, which frequently besets the church, of deifying itself and of giving the sanction of religion to an historical culture, it is always open to confusing its own social and moral vision with the Kingdom of God. It fails to appreciate the meaning of the sacramental life.

THE CHURCH IN WORSHIP

The Protestant Reformation was a churchly movement. It was not the protest of individualists and pietists; it was largely a revolt against the individualism of the late Middle Ages. The

Reformers had a clear grasp of the corporate nature of Christian life and worship. Indeed, so basic was this to the Reformation that the Church became defined from the point of view of worship. Where the Word of God is preached and the two sacraments are administered, there is the Church. Not its papal organisation or its hierarchy, but its fellowship in worship, is its distinguishing characteristic. It is of course true that a certain type of individualism underlay the principle of the Reformation. It expressed itself in the belief that men should trust their consciences, guided by the spirit of God, rather than obey the established authority of the Roman Church. On the limits of this right of private judgment the Reformers were far from agreed. Calvin in particular liked to assert his interpretation of Holy Scripture as an infallible authority. Yet the Westminster Confession is perhaps most true to the principle of the Reformation when it asserts, "God is alone Lord of the conscience."

The Reformers produced a great variety of forms for the conduct of worship, but they are characterised by a certain general agreement. The liturgies of the Reformation are firstly distinguished by their feeling for corporate worship. They recovered what the late Middle Ages with the cult of the Reserved Sacrament and the stress on the elevation had tended to neglect—the vital sense of Christian worship as an act of united devotion and service. The people of God meet to praise Him and to offer their prayers and thanksgivings together. This sense of corporate worship is heightened by the introduction of the vernacular and of hymn singing, in which the congregation can take part. The elaborate chants of the monks and of trained choirs are set aside for simple popular tunes, in which all can join. The service, rendered in the language of the people, becomes intelligible. Instead of witnessing with their eyes a drama that could so easily

lead to superstition, men could grasp with their minds the meaning of the Scriptures and could appreciate the prayers voiced by
the minister as the representative of the congregation. Finally,
the Reformers were insistent upon the demand that all the faithful should communicate at the Lord's Supper. The medieval
custom of very infrequent communion they deplored, for they
regarded the united fellowship of the congregation with Christ
as the profoundest meaning of the sacrament. They restored the
cup to the laity (denied them since the thirteenth century) in
order more fully to bring out the original significance of the
Lord's Supper as corporate table fellowship with Christ.

The second characteristic of the Reformation worship was
its didactic interest. This was a timely and much-needed emphasis but soon came to be overstressed. Such a passion did
Luther have for the element of instruction in worship that he
wanted the Mass said on alternate Sundays in Hebrew, Greek,
Latin, and German for the edification of the people. Yet there
was a basic need that the people should be told what the gospel
was, what God demanded of men and had accomplished for
them in Christ. The intellectual element in worship cannot be
neglected without grave peril, for men cannot truly worship in
a mystic trance that ends in nothingness.

This stress upon instruction had a prophetic foundation. The
Reformers witnessed to the living God, to the reality of His
redemption in Jesus Christ. They had a vital message for their
age, to deny the corruption and superstition of the Latin Church,
to break through its sophistry and legislative paraphernalia, in
order to find the abounding mercy and grace of God. It was the
vitality, the urgency, and insistency of this gospel that impelled
the Reformers to give preaching the predominant rank it has
held ever since in the Protestant churches.

From some points of view this emphasis on preaching led to a grave defect in Protestant worship. It elevated the minister's private opinions to an abnormal place. Not seldom the congregation was "preached at." They came to hear sermons rather than actively to worship God. Finally, when ministers lacked a real gospel of power such as Luther and Calvin had preached, they devoted their sermons to secular topics and to interesting but hardly vital subjects. This is the danger always inherent in Protestantism that presupposes the minister has a prophetic mission.

A third feature of Reformation worship was its denial of the Mass as the actual sacrifice of Christ re-enacted by the priest. The Reformers regarded the medieval conception as nothing short of blasphemous. They refused to admit that the priest could mediate between the people and God by the sacrifice of the body and blood of Christ. They emphasised that the meaning of the Lord's Supper was fellowship with Christ. The only sacrifice in Protestant worship was that "of ourselves, our souls and bodies," which were offered to God for His service. Again the Reformers did the Christian liturgy a timely service, but they lost the richness of the primitive Eucharist and of the Roman Mass. They neglected the idea that the sacramental elements were an offering to God, symbolising the complete self-giving of His people, who associated themselves with the perfect offering of Christ for the sin of the world. The Reformers were naturally hesitant to use any sacrificial language of the bread and wine, fearing that the interpretation of the Roman Mass would again creep in. While we may sympathise with their predicament, we cannot deny that they deprived the Eucharist of something of its deepest meaning.

In general, Protestant worship followed the lines laid down

by the early Reformers, but with one very significant difference. Both Luther and Calvin insisted that the Lord's Supper should be the central Sunday service. Here they were true to the long liturgical tradition of Christianity. Despite their abhorrence of the Roman Mass nothing was further from their thought than that the Eucharist should become a neglected rite. In this regard much modern Protestantism is totally unfaithful to its founders. They strove to reform Christian worship and to give the central service something of its primitive meaning. The earliest German and French liturgies of the Reformation are not attempts to construct services purely of preaching and prayer, but they are translations and adaptations of the Roman Mass. Their writers tried to eliminate what they thought was unsound doctrine and to recover the original significance of the Eucharistic rite, but they wanted it as basic to Christian worship. It is not only from the medieval service of Prone but from the mass itself that the German and Reformed rites are ultimately derived.

Yet the Reformers were unable to carry out their original intentions. Both Luther and Calvin found the people and the magistrates opposed to frequent celebrations of the Communion. Some of this opposition doubtless arose from the abhorrence with which Protestants regarded the Roman Mass. Much of it was due to the fact that the people were unused to communicating frequently and hence preferred a service of preaching and prayer to the weekly Eucharist. More and more this became a practical necessity as the Reformers refused to have the Lord's Supper unless the congregation fully participated. Following this trend the Genevan magistrates forced upon the Church quarterly communion, despite the insistent protest of Calvin himself.

The infrequent communion in modern Protestant churches goes back to this development, which departed from the general liturgical tradition of Christianity. The Sunday service of prayer and preaching has become characteristic of Protestantism. Nevertheless, even this service reflects something of its original meaning. In its origin it really represents the first part of the Mass —the Mass of the Catechumens, as it was called. In the Eastern Church, whose liturgies had some influence on the Reformation rites, the service was sharply divided into two parts. The first contained the reading of Scripture and various prayers, and at this the unbaptised could be present. In the second half came the consecration and administration of the elements, and in this part of the service only the baptised were allowed to participate. It is really from this first half of the Mass that the distinctively Protestant form of Sunday worship is derived.

This is not, however, true of the service of Morning Prayer, which in many Anglican churches since the eighteenth century[6] has superseded the office of the Holy Communion as the central eleven o'clock Sunday service. Morning Prayer is derived from the choir offices of the Middle Ages, i.e., the daily services of prayer and Scripture reading said by the monks throughout the week. It is noteworthy that the structure of Morning Prayer has basically affected many recent revisions of the liturgy, especially in the Church of Scotland.

The liturgies produced by the Lutheran, Calvinistic, and Anglican churches preserve some of the distinctive features of these three movements within Protestantism. The Lutheran forms are marked by a warm personal religion and emphasise the reality of the presence of Christ in the Eucharist and the deep experience of God's forgiveness through Him. The Calvinistic liturgies stress

---

[6]During this period Holy Communion was administered generally on the first Sunday of the month, which came to be called "Sacrament Sunday." The most recent trend in the Anglican Church is to restore the Eucharist as a central morning service of corporate worship.

the glory and transcendent majesty of God, before whom man is awed and realises his sinful nature. This sense is well reflected in the long opening prayer of confession in the Genevan and Scottish rites, while the moral earnestness of Calvinism is uniquely expressed in the stress upon the Ten Commandments. The Anglican rite preserves a happy union of Protestant and Catholic elements, and the liturgical language of the Book of Common Prayer is perhaps the finest that the Reformation produced. It is marked by grave but simple dignity and its beautiful cadences have never been surpassed. In its theology it is neither clear nor consistent, but in its spiritual depth it betrays rare insight. It is the classic document which reveals the genius of the English Reformation.

Finally, there were those churches like the Congregational and Baptist, which preferred to reject all liturgical forms and to leave the conduct of the service to the free discretion of the minister. This type of worship was characterised by the singing of hymns or psalms, and by the reading of Scripture, while preaching and lengthy extempore prayer played a predominant rôle. At the Eucharist even to recite the words of institution was not deemed an absolute necessity. The spirit of liturgical freedom reached its climax among the Quakers, who rejected all sacraments and stressed silence as the most perfect form of worship. The earnest religious life of these Reformation sects prevented their services from ending in chaos or levity. Indeed, the very freedom of their worship gave it a heightened sense of serious responsibility. In later years, however, there grew up a tendency to abide by some fixed order of service and even to adopt liturgical forms of prayer, a trend among Congregationalists, Baptists, and other Free churches which is particularly evident today.

On first thought it might be imagined that the characteristically

Protestant service was barren in the extreme. We are accustomed to think of the church structure with its predominant pulpit and its simple communion table, and the minister with his black gown. We note the vivid contrast they make with the rich ornaments of the medieval Mass. The priestly vestments, the images, candles, and pictures are dramatic and colourful beside the drab appearance of Protestant worship. Yet it must not be forgotten that the Reformers were often conservative in the changes they made in medieval ritual. In many Lutheran churches, for instance, the old vestments were retained and Luther himself only abolished the elevation in 1542. The Anglican development was similar, and while the Genevan influence was predominant by 1552, the effort was made to enforce the use of the cassock and surplice as a minimum. Even in Geneva, the centre of the Puritan emphasis on simplicity, it must not be overlooked that the recovery of the vernacular, the stress on congregational singing and vital preaching, largely compensated for the loss of the dramatic ritual of the medieval Church.

CHAPTER VII

THE CHURCH IN THE LIFE AND THOUGHT
OF THE MODERN PERIOD

THE ENLIGHTENMENT

MODERN thinking about the Church, especially in America, has its roots more in the Enlightenment than in the developments of classical Protestantism. In America we think of the churches as a vast number of different denominations and sects, comprising some two hundred varieties according to the last census. They are essentially voluntary associations of believers, who bind themselves together to worship God according to their tradition and taste. At the root of this conception lies the most characteristic idea of the Enlightenment—toleration.

The German Enlightenment was a revolt against authority in the interests of the scientific or critical point of view. Its presupposition was that knowledge, to be accounted as truth, must be verified with the precision of mathematical and scientific experiment. Knowledge was empirical knowledge, derived from the experience of the senses. It was subject to measurement and its truth could be accurately tested by critical examination. Reason, the common possession of all men, was the final authority, and the idea of revelation was relegated to a place of inferior, if of any, importance.

The rise of this kind of thinking, which really stems from the philosophy of Descartes, was largely due to the long wars of religion, which devastated Germany and other parts of Europe.

Religious authority and the concept of revelation, upon which it rested, seemed to be the source of endless human misery and degradation, instead of the assurance of man's salvation. Furthermore, there was much to justify the revolt against ecclesiastical authority. The deep faith and religious sensitivity of the early Reformers like Luther had largely passed away. In its place there was to be found a kind of petrified orthodoxy, in which faith was reduced to a number of propositions, supposedly based on the divine sanction of the Scriptures.[1] It was a poor substitute for the idea of faith basic to the Reformers, the dynamic power or Word of God. This Protestant intellectualism had many affinities with the scholasticism of the Middle Ages and produced a religious revolt, in some ways not unlike the Reformation itself. This was Pietism, a movement led by Spener and Francke in Germany, elements of which came into England through the influence of John Wesley and into America with the Great Awakening. While Pietism lacked the deep sense of corporate Christian life which we have noted in the early Reformers, nevertheless, it did recover something of the religious earnestness and inwardness of the Reformation. It was an individualistic movement, where concern for personal religious experience often found expression in a morbid dwelling upon the state of the soul, and tended to reduce religion to subjective feeling. Yet its very enthusiasm made Christianity real, and prevented relegating it to the arid discussions of theologians and to barren dogmatic statements. Pietism never gained many lasting adherents, but its individualism and its revolt against ecclesiastical authority paved

[1]The tendency to define the Church as the number of those who assent to correct intellectual propositions about the Faith was something which Luther himself did not altogether escape. After the tragic debates at the Marburg Colloquy (1529), in which the irreconcilable differences between Luther and Zwingli on the doctrine of the Lord's Supper had been clearly brought out, Luther published his Schwabach Articles. In these he stated: "The Church is nothing else than believers in Christ who hold, believe and teach the above enumerated articles."

the way for the Enlightenment, in which the importance of the individual and of human reason were stressed against the divine authority claimed by the Roman and Protestant Churches.

Reason demanded that men should cease to wage war in the interests of special forms of religion and for the sake of dogmas, whose verity could not be attested with the precision of science. As far as religion was concerned, the men of the Enlightenment reduced it to the fewest possible principles, which were regarded as the natural possession of all men and of all religions. Just as the natural law was the basis of their social life, so it was imagined there was a natural religion which all men recognised in one form or another. Its particular expressions were matters of indifference; taste and tradition could account for them. The only important thing was that men should be willing to abide by the generally accepted principles of morality, recognising that God would judge them if they failed to do their duty. The most profound conviction of Paul, that man was incapable of doing the law imposed upon him by God, was neglected and not understood. An optimistic view of man's nature and capacity was in the ascendant. Man's obligations were defined, not from the point of view of what God required by His Revelation, but of what man was capable of accomplishing, if only he set himself to do it. It was regarded as axiomatic that most men were normally decent and were motivated by "benevolent sympathy."

The same type of individualism and optimism was equally evident in other realms. In economics Adam Smith propounded his famous theory of capitalism, in which he contended that the general welfare of the nation is inevitably advanced by the aggressive activity of the individual in business, unhampered by the laws of the State. In philosophy Leibnitz talked about "monads," little self-sufficient entities, moving about in a pre-established harmony. This type of thinking was definitely unhistorical. It did not appreciate the meaning of crisis. It imagined that man was set in a world favourable to individual activity. The State was looked upon as an umpire in a general game of advancing individual interests. Its duty was not to make laws, which interfered with economics or imposed upon its citizens a definite religious obligation. It was believed that the pre-established harmony of the world would look after the general welfare of the nation, if all the citizens worked hard to better their own positions. Except in enforcing the general moral precepts upon which all social life is based, the State should have no concern with religion. Religious belief was a matter for free and private opinion. Churches were voluntary associations of men, "joining themselves together of their own accord, in order to the public worshiping of God in such a manner as they may judge acceptable to Him and effectual to the salvation of their souls," as the English philosopher, John Locke, expressed it.

Out of this development grew the modern idea of the denomination, which is neither a sect nor a church in the strict sense of these words. The sects were marked by their exclusiveness and the voluntary basis of their association. Many of them, as the Donatists of old, claimed to be the only true Church, and all of them were characterised by a strict and austere morality, in contrast to the lax life of the established churches. The "churches," on the other hand, were distinguished by their close association with the secular power, and by their belief that religious institutions carried on the traditional faith and sacraments, independent of the morality of their adherents. Though the early Reformers had derived much of the force and success of their revolt against Rome from their exposure of the moral corruption of the medieval Church and of its priests, nevertheless, neither

Luther nor Calvin ever held that the moral life of the minister could vitiate the power of the sacrament or invalidate the Church's ministrations.

What we mean by the term denomination really incorporates both sectarian and churchly elements, but its basic characteristic is the idea of toleration, derived from the Enlightenment. It is sectarian in that its adherents are united by free association: it is churchly insofar as it claims to carry on a traditional institution with dogma and sacraments. It is uniquely the child of the Enlightenment, in that it regards other forms of Christian organisation with toleration, and looks upon them as fellow companies of Christian believers. To a limited extent this attitude of tolerance had been true of the great churches of the Reformation. The Calvinists in Geneva, the Lutherans in Germany, and the Anglicans in England, tended to look upon one another as sister churches. While they deplored the corruptions of Rome, both Hooker and Calvin admitted that some Romanists might be true Christians. Calvin had even conceived the idea of a united, world-wide Protestant Church, which would have something of the universal character of the Roman Church, while being based upon a Reformed creed. Such an idea never made any practical progress and was doomed to failure. The Protestant Reformation in most countries was too closely allied with the independent, national spirit of the age. Furthermore, such an organisation was impossible, because Calvin was adamant in his dogma of the Presbyterian ministry as the only one sanctioned by Scripture.

With the Enlightenment, and particularly in America after the Union, this incipient toleration was given a surer foundation. The various Protestant churches came to regard each other as fellow companies of Christians. While they held that each denomination, by virtue of its own traditions and background, might have a special contribution to make, the unity of their Christian devotion was looked upon as of more consequence than their divergent forms and organisations. Religion was held to be a voluntary practice and was regarded more as a helpful way of rounding out life and giving it fuller expression, than as its very foundation and meaning. This widespread trend of toleration had grave consequences. It led often to indifference and to disregarding the vital historical elements, which had originally divided the churches. In its deepest significance toleration should mean humility, and should prevent any single organisation or interpretation of Christianity from setting itself up as the sole mouthpiece of God. But indifference is the degradation of true toleration. It is based, as Francis Bacon—that shrewd and careful essayist—once remarked, upon a false unity that finds all colours look alike in the dark. It has no part in vital religion. Christianity involves decision and determination to pursue the will of God as we see it in the corporate life and faith of the Christian community. Yet it also involves humility, and sees that all human activity stands under the judgment of God and falls short of His Glory.

Under the impetus of the thinking of the Enlightenment, the former close association of the secular power with the churches gave way to the idea of complete separation. Christianity was conceived of as a voluntary practice, and the churches were looked upon as free associations for worship. Hence it was not the duty of the State actively to support any church. The ultimate end of secular government was not conceived in religious terms. The State claimed its complete independence of religion. It recognised no duty or obligation to promote Christianity, nor did it believe that the exercise of its power rested upon a divine sanction.

This idea had sad results. Religion was looked upon as an independent department of life—to be thought of in the same way as politics, economics, education or any other aspect of man's existence. Each was an isolated, independent whole, and all were on the same level. Science was independent of religion: art was divorced from politics. Thus life was broken up into isolated fragments, and lacked any cohesive unity. This contrasted very clearly with the medieval view, in which the various aspects of man's life were caught up into a living whole in the Church, and Christianity was believed to be the foundation of all existence. It set the goal for all social life. It was the ground of all meaning in life. Not a little of the distress of our modern age arises from the fact that our civilisation lacks cohesive unity. It has arisen from a development which failed to recognise that religion is concerned with the ultimate meaning of life, and is the only basis upon which a unified social order can be created. Religion is not a department of life along with politics or education: it is the ground and end of human existence.

Yet the chief Protestant denominations of America have not been without profound influence upon the trend of modern social life. If the conception of religion as revelation has been neglected, their vigour in asserting the moral duties of life has been the more insistent. The "social gospel" with its activism in the abolition of slavery, in demanding social legislation, and in the less fruitful prohibition experiment, has won many notable triumphs, and has raised the moral tone of American life. It has expressed in social terms the same basic austerity that marked the individualistic ethics of the sects. In its most extreme expression this type of moralistic religion has produced a radical socialistic Christianity, which is vitally concerned about the working and living conditions of the underprivileged, and has actively participated in the cause of justice. Many of these developments have their roots in the ethics of the Enlightenment, and the Protestant denominations have often become the guardians of American Ideals, rather than of traditional forms of Christianity. Nevertheless, this activity of the American churches has not lacked an earnest religious vigour, centred in the Christian faith.

ROMAN CATHOLICISM

The Roman Church has always remained faithful to the medieval ideal. The rise of nationalism did not alter its theory of Church and State, though practical necessity prevented its realisation. Its philosophy did not change with the Enlightenment, and its ethics were not seriously affected by the rise either of capitalism or communism. Of recent days papal encyclicals have condemned both the "unbridled ambition" of capitalism and the anti-religious propaganda of Marxism. To preserve its existence the Roman Church has largely allied itself with Fascism. It has denounced all forms of communism, not only because it is anti-Christian, but because it renounces private property, which the Roman Church regards as a God-given institution for society.

After the Reformation the Roman Church put its house in order at the Council of Trent (1545 to 1563), and corrected many of its corruptions and abuses. The growing power of Protestantism was counterbalanced by a new semi-monastic movement which was vigorously aggressive and rigidly disciplined. It had as its ideal not retirement from the world, but close association with every aspect of the world's life in order to conquer it for the Church. The founder of the Jesuits was Ignatius Loyola, who died in 1556. This Spanish soldier, whose fall from his horse prevented his pursuing military service, diverted the ambition and the fiery zeal (so characteristic of the Spanish temperament) to the cause of the Church. The spiritual soldiers of his order did much to recover the prestige of the papacy. Although in their methods the Jesuits became proverbial for their casuistry, by which any means, no mater how dubious, was justified by the end, their devotion and spiritual ardour cannot be called in question. The *Spiritual Exercises* of Ignatius Loyola are a classic of disciplined piety. Though highly individualistic in tone, they reflect the austerity and religious earnestness of the order at its best.

In their theory of the Church the Romanists have remained true to the idea of the divine institution centred in the papacy. They acknowledge "the Holy Catholic Apostolic Roman Church for the mother and mistress of all churches," and insist upon obedience to the Bishop of Rome, who is the "successor to Saint Peter, Prince of Apostles and Vicar of Jesus Christ." They did, however, elaborate a more clear doctrine which tried to meet the problem set by the Reformers in their distinction of Church visible and invisible. Largely under the influence of the theologian Bellarmine (d. 1621), the classic definition of the soul and body of the Church was given.

The metaphor is originally taken from Augustine, but the developed statement is more elaborate. It is contended that the Church, like any living organism, has a body and a soul. By the former is meant the visible organisation, distinguished by the four marks which Augustine laid down, unity, catholicity, apostolicity, and sanctity. By the soul are meant the internal gifts of the Church, grace, faith, and love, without which no one can attain salvation. Not all in the actual, visible body have appropriated these divine gifts: indeed, within it there may be heretics and blasphemers. On the other hand, there may be some outside the body who really belong to the soul. They may have been prevented from joining the actual visible Church through blindness or intellectual ignorance, but, because God has favoured them with His grace, they will be saved. Their spiritual life, indeed, is immature, since they have not shared in the Church's sacraments. Nevertheless, by virtue of God's grace they can in a sense be said to belong potentially to the body, for it is the purpose of God's grace to bring men unto the Church, which is an organic whole—soul and body together. They thus belong to the Church by intention, by desire (*voto*), though the desire may not be clearly apprehended in this life or reach its final expression in communion with the visible Roman Church. Hence, with the recognition that baptism confers some grace of God, Pope Pius IX stated in an encyclical (1873), "Every one who has received baptism belongs somehow to the Pope," and such persons, "though far from the visible centre, have a special claim to our love." In this way, then, the absolute identification of the visible Roman Church with the body of God's people is avoided, while the organic unity of the Church is preserved.

This sense of unity is most completely seen in the definition of papal infallibility in 1870, an incident of grave and dramatic significance. On the 18th of July, 1870, amid one of the darkest and most violent storms experienced in Rome, the Pope declared to the world his infallibility, when speaking *ex cathedra* on matters of faith and morals. On this dramatic day it is said that darkness seemed to fill Saint Peter's, and was only alleviated by the intermittent flashes of lightning. After the bishops, with only two exceptions, had voted affirmatively to the decision, the moment came for the Pope himself to read the decree. In the general gloom and darkness only his golden mitre seemed visible, and a servitor had to be called to hold a lighted candle so that the Pope could read the declaration of his own infallibility. When he had concluded, the applause of the bishops mingled with the claps of thunder. The Pope had claimed the divine attribute and summed up the long development of papal authority since the days of the Council of Sardica. Two anxious months intervened. Then King Victor Emmanuel hammered at the doors of Rome, depriving the papacy of its temporal power, and making the Pope a virtual exile in the lands that for so long had been the independent possession of the Church. Eighteen-seventy was indeed a pregnant year—papal infallibility and the unification of Italy! The Pope had declared his divine spiritual might at the very moment when the political policy pursued by his predecessors for a thousand years had been finally defeated. Though the Concordat with Mussolini, in 1929, restored to the papacy a limited portion of its original possessions, its powerful voice in international diplomacy has been somewhat tempered by its close proximity to the domineering Fascist State.

METHODISM

Methodism was a unique development. It attempted to combine two religious trends, which had formerly stood in marked opposition. While it stressed a vital personal religion of the Pietist type, laying great emphasis upon the experience of conversion, it was organised into a closely knit and elaborate institution. John Wesley (d. 1791), its founder, was himself a man of remarkable ability. To his profound religious faith and deep personal piety he brought a unique genius for organisation. These gifts are seldom found together and their successful combination is an exceptional achievement. Methodism owes its most distinctive feature, and not a little of its success, to this rare quality of its founder.

In its origins Methodism was a revolt against the general spirit of the Enlightenment in eighteenth-century England. It stressed vital, personal religion in contrast to the cold rationalism of that epoch. It preached Christianity as a living experience and not as a moral code or an obsolete dogma. It had fervour and conviction in an age that looked askance at all forms of enthusiasm and emotionalism. As a movement born within the Church of England it sought to revitalise ancient forms and traditions, and to make Christianity a vital way of life to nominal members of the Church. But it also had a fervent missionary zeal, and reached thousands uncared for by the established Church. Methodism coincided with the beginnings of the Industrial Revolution. Hosts of the poorer classes flocked to the growing towns, and the ancient parochial system of the Church of England could not easily adapt itself to meet these new conditions. The early Methodists were not unlike the Franciscans of the thirteenth century: they were an urban religious movement, preaching the gospel to multitudes whom the Church did not meet with its ministrations.

Methodism had prophetic ardour and simple conviction. It preached to poor and unlettered people, such as the colliers of Kingswood, and it preached so that they could understand. It convicted them of sin, assured them of grace, and witnessed to the Cross of Christ. It united men in small groups, where they examined themselves with religious earnestness. They confessed their sins together: they told each other of their simple spiritual triumphs. They had a vivid sense of corporate Christian life. They shared in each other's virtues and prayed for each other's failings. In practical ways no less than in spiritual the Methodists helped one another. By an organised system of charity they aided those in dire poverty. But they went further: they found them work. They aided each other in business. Methodists traded with Methodists and they employed one another wherever possible.

Methodism brought a religious self-confidence and a measure

of practical independence to men who had been looked down upon as the "lower classes." It taught them diligence in work and frugality in pleasure. It impressed upon them simple virtues, such as honesty, sobriety, purity, cleanliness, and saving for a rainy day. In its preaching and its practice it was peculiarly adapted to the lower classes among whom it found an immediate and enduring appeal. Its preachers were similarly drawn from the ranks of skilled artisans, small tradesmen, and farmers.

Wesley had been born and bred a Tory and a High Churchman of the eighteenth century. He was an advanced ritualist, given to fasting and to other religious observances. But his disciplined life which he shared with other young men in the Holy Club at Oxford,[2] included a variety of social work. He visited prisons, released debtors, provided a fund to feed destitute families, and founded a poor school. In his politics he was a Tory, devoted to the King and firmly convinced that the best government was autocratic. In his churchmanship he was thoroughly loyal to the establishment, and believed implicitly in episcopacy as the divinely appointed constitution of the Church. Thus in his early life Wesley was scrupulous in his opinions, disciplined in his conduct, and liberal in his charity.

The turning point of his career was his conversion on May 24, 1738. He wrote, "I felt my heart strangely warmed. I felt I did trust in Christ, Christ alone for salvation; and an assurance was given me that he had taken away *my* sins, even *mine,* and saved me from the law of sin and death." It was this experience, growing out of his contact with the German Pietists (the Moravians) and with the religious societies in England (which had not been uninfluenced by this German movement), that dominated his

---

[2]In its origin the term Methodist was a derisive nickname applied to these young men because of their discipline and methodical life.

whole life and contributed vigour and vital conviction to his religious activity. But while the Methodist movement was rooted in this Pietistic experience, its organisation and its practical disciplines go back to his training as a Tory and a High Churchman. Wesley ruled the Methodist Societies with the same autocratic and paternal authority that he advocated in kings, and his General Rules for the Societies reflect the ordered and disciplined conduct of the Holy Club. They are marked, indeed, by an absence of those scrupulous ecclesiastical rules that dominated his early life, but their simple and austere morality none the less evidences the legal temper of his mind.

Methodism began as an effort to revitalise the life of the English Church, by stressing the experience of Christian conversion and the practical duties of Christian conduct. It was meant to be churchly and had as its aim to supplement, not to supersede, the Church's ministrations. Wesley forbade his preachers to celebrate the sacraments: they were to be "extraordinary messengers raised up to provoke the ordinary ones to jealousy." Theirs was a prophetic, not a priestly office. They were not to rival the clergy of the established Church. The people called "Methodists" were to regard themselves as of no particular party or sect. They were to be recruited from all churches, Dissenters and Conformists alike. But they were to retain their loyalty to their own denominations. Their only bond of unity was to be "the real desire to flee from the wrath to come."

Yet Methodism ultimately resulted in separation. Although Wesley again and again asserted that he was true to the established Church, he really initiated a schism. Toward the end of his life he declared, "I live and die a member of the Church of England." He was equally insistent that "when the Methodists leave the Church of England God would leave them." Yet out of his life work there grew one of the most powerful churches of the English-speaking world. A large part of the blame may lie with the bishops and clergy of the English Church, who neither shared any enthusiasm for his movement nor offered him any co-operation. Frequently the parish clergy denied the sacrament to Methodists, and even stirred up popular opposition and riots against Wesley and his preachers. The general attitude of the Church was well reflected in a remark of Bishop Butler, "This pretending to extraordinary revelation and gifts of the Holy Ghost is a horrid thing, a very horrid thing." It is not surprising, however, that the Church should have looked askance at Wesley and his lay preachers, who were invading the parishes of England and forming their converts into little bands, which had a wide but closely knit organisation, summed up in Wesley himself.

The opposition and indifference of the clergy to his movement hastened the separation. Wesley had to build chapels of his own, and finally to hold Sunday services during the regular hours of worship, a practice which he at first sternly opposed. With its itinerant preachers, classes, bands, and quarterly meetings, Methodism developed an elaborate organisation. The preachers were even forced at times to take out dissenting licenses, in order to conform to the Conventicle Act, which forbade the use of unlicensed chapels for public worship. The separation came to a head in the ordinations of 1784. Several years before Wesley had been convinced that the terms presbyter and bishop were synonyms in the New Testament. Hence he, as a presbyter of the Church of England, claimed the right to ordain. When every attempt to persuade the English bishops to ordain his preachers for work in America had failed, he determined to exercise the right himself. He ordained Whatcoate and Vasey as elders and "set aside" Doctor Coke as "superintendent." Within two years he ordained seven more presbyters, including three for work in England. Thus the canon of the Church of England, that only bishops have the power to ordain, had been flatly disobeyed. After this, Wesley's claim to be a faithful member of the Church of England was hardly convincing. Though he tried to justify his action on the grounds of expedience and the urgent necessity of the work in America, he had really demonstrated that Methodism meant dissent.

At heart Wesley had a different conception of the nature of the Church from that of the establishment. He held that, since unworthy clergy and bishops could not be true spiritual governors, they had no real ecclesiastical power, but only a temporal authority derived from the King. Therefore he claimed the right to override their decisions, when the gospel was at stake. He asserted that obedience was due to bishops only in matters of indifference. He even disregarded the rubrics of the Prayer Book, which he once claimed were binding on him as a Church of England minister. Indeed, he came to look upon the Church of England as a mere political institution, while the true Church was the body of those whom God had called out of the world and were united by one faith and by a life of moral holiness.

Wesley's doctrine of the ministry was essentially authoritative. He held that presbyters received the right to exercise their priestly functions as ministers of the sacraments by virtue of their ordination, the authority of which reached back in long succession to the Apostles. As well as the priestly, there was also the prophetic ministry. These prophets were the extraordinary messengers of God, whom He raised up directly. Of such Wesley came to regard himself. As an administrator, however, he tended to consider that the lay preachers, whom he appointed to this prophetic calling, owed their commission to him, and must render him implicit obedience. This double concept of the ministry, as priestly and prophetic, well characterises the genius of Methodism, with its strong sense of institutionalism and its stress upon individual religious experience.

Though the Methodists became separated from the Church of England, they did not form a sect. They retained many aspects of their Anglican heritage, notably the liturgy, which was not radically changed. They held to an elaborate and very autocratic organisation, presided over by the paternal spirit of its founder. In later days the same high-handed policy was pursued by Jabez Bunting, who earned the title of the "Pope of Methodism." There was nothing purely individualistic about the religion of Wesley and his successors. He himself had once written that "Holy Solitaries" were no more consistent with the Gospel than "Holy Adulterers . . . the Gospel of Christ knows of no religion but social; no Holiness but Social Holiness." Thus Methodism combined institutionalism with individualism in a remarkable way, stressing at once the necessity of personal religion and the obligation of Church membership. Churchly and social duties were no less typical of the movement than the vivid experience of conversion.

It was, however, extremely difficult to guard these two poles of Methodism—personal religion and institutionalism. Through the course of its history the movement tended to disintegrate, and various groups broke from the parent body as early as 1797. These secessions were largely due to the influence of liberal ideas about government. A more democratic constitution was demanded for the Church, and a more radical attitude was taken toward politics. With his Tory allegiance Wesley had been firmly opposed to the liberal and democratic sentiments, which had penetrated England from a variety of sources. The English Dissenters, who were the main support of the Whigs in politics, had learned something of democracy from John Calvin, while the French Revolution and the declaration of American independence had not been without influence upon English political life. The groups who seceded from the original Methodists were largely those who had become inoculated with popular political radicalism, and had pressed the dissenting principle to its logical conclusion. They opposed the autocratic rule which had been established by Wesley and had been exercised after his death by the Legal Hundred. Furthermore, the close contact of many of the Methodist preachers with the poorer people had made them keenly aware of the need of political reform. Thus they allied themselves with various causes of political agitation, while the original Methodist Societies remained reactionary. The latter were insistent that religion and politics had no clear relationship, save that the Christian should be obedient to the ruling powers. The Kingdom, they claimed, was not of this world. Thus they looked upon their seceding brethren as "dupes of faction," for to them the sedition and rebellion that seemed to be fostered by the growing liberalism were essentially sinful.

The great success of Methodism in America, where it became one of the leading Protestant churches, was due to the same combination of individualism and institutionalism. On the frontier it offered a vital religion, grounded in personal experience, and robbed of the sophistication and tradition of the established churches in the East. Furthermore, the highly centralised Methodist polity was able to provide the West swiftly and efficiently with bands of itinerant preachers. The advanced social interests of a section of the modern Methodist Church in America have their roots in the same sense of social duty that marked the earlier English secessions. A keen sense of ethical obligation is rooted in Methodism—whether this is interpreted in the form of that personal discipline and conduct stressed in Wesley's Rules, or whether it is viewed in its wider social implications of political radicalism. Personal religion and social duty have, in one form or another, always been at the basis of the Methodist idea of the Church. It is conceived of as a closely knit body of believers, bound together by a common religious experience, and by the duties of Christian conduct.

ANGLICANISM

Among Anglicans many diverse doctrines of the Church are held. This is only natural, since the Church of England was built upon the double foundation of Catholicism and Protestantism. While the *via media* position of Richard Hooker is perhaps most typical of the English temperament, both Catholic and Protestant extremes have been found within Anglicanism. The Methodist Revival of the eighteenth century, while finally separating from the Church, had nevertheless great effect upon it. Its evangelical emphasis upon personal religion has largely characterised the Low Church party, which derives originally from the puritan influence of the sixteenth century.

It is, however, the more Catholic trend which has been in the ascendant since the Oxford Movement of the nineteenth century. This movement was a churchly protest against secular domination. It tried to recover the sense of the Church as an institution independent of the State and resting its claim to authority upon its divine foundation. The first outcry of the Oxford Tractarians was precipitated by the attempt of Parliament, in the Church Temporalities Act, to suppress a number of Irish bishoprics, and reduce the ecclesiastical revenues. That this was a measure of practical wisdom from the point of view of the government can hardly be denied. It was one factor in a long struggle that finally ended in the disestablishment of the Irish Church in 1868—the only possible solution of the problem, since the majority of the Irish were Roman Catholics. Keble's Assize Sermon on the National Apostasy, protesting this interference of the State, was a challenge to the Church to examine its nature and the foundations of its authority.

The movement that resulted was an attempt to free the Church from the secular bondage into which it had fallen, and to assert the independence of its life and authority from the State. The general trend during the last two centuries had been to regard the Church as the state department of religion, and the very fact that Convocation had been suppressed since 1717 showed that the Church had fallen upon evil days. The liberal emphasis, rooted in the Enlightenment and in the growth of toleration, made further difficulties for the Church. Many churchmen, among them Doctor Arnold, contended that, if the established Church was to have any significance, it must be united with all other denominations in England in a minimum Christianity. This policy was maliciously criticised by a High Churchman who wrote, "Arnold proposed that all denominations should be united by Act of Parliament with the Church of England on the principle of retaining all their distinctive errors and absurdities." It was against this liberal toleration that often amounted to indifference, no less than against secular domination, that the Oxford Movement revolted.

The doctrine of the Church, which gained particular prominence in the writings of the Oxford Tractarians, was that of Apostolical Succession. This was by no means new in Anglicanism. It had found frequent expression, especially during the period of the Caroline divines, the classic theologians of the Church of England in the seventeenth century. In its most uncompromising definition it affirmed that the validity of the sacraments and teaching of the Church depended upon the unbroken succession of an order of bishops, distinct from presbyters. These bishops, it was contended, were by their consecration the successors of the apostles and owed their authority directly to Jesus Christ, the Founder of the Church. In order to appreciate this doctrine as it was defined in the seventeenth century, we must turn back to consider the question of episcopacy in the English Church during the Reformation.

It is interesting that, in the earliest stages of the Puritan struggle, episcopacy was defended as a wise and legitimate historical development, rather than as an immutable type of Church government, established by divine right. It was the Puritans, and not the Anglicans, who first contended that there was only one prescribed form of polity for the Christian Church. With their customary gloomy intolerance they upheld their presbyterian order as the sole type sanctioned by divine law, and nothing would have pleased them more than to have enforced it upon the whole Church. All their efforts were devoted to this end and presbyterianism became in their minds a panacea for all the evils of Christendom.

In replying to them, a number of Anglican writers contended that no single polity could claim absolute divine approval to the exclusion of others. With true political shrewdness they held that Church organisation was a matter of tradition and historical relevance, and was not to be regulated by divine laws supposedly derived from scripture. Indeed, Hooker, with his usual judiciousness, explained that no single rule of Church government is clearly laid down in Holy Scripture, and he upheld episcopacy by showing it was established by tradition, convenient in practice, and in no way contrary to God's Word. Moreover, it seemed to him the type of polity, "which best agreeth with the sacred Scripture." Hooker was typically English. He was conservative; he loved tradition, and he hated political panaceas. He was fearful of any sudden revelations which would determine the course of human events by biblical rules-of-thumb or fanatical oversimplifications. He would not ride rough-shod over the traditions and facts of history. He was quite aware, as were the medieval theologians since Jerome, that *episcopos* and *presbyteros* are synonyms in the New Testament, and that mon-episcopacy was an historical development. He held that the peculiar power of bishops arose through the need for order and peace in the Church, and that the period of equal presbyters lasted only while the apostles were there to control them. When this exercise of authority was no longer possible, they dedicated their powers to successors, who held a place of prominence in the government of the Church, and for whom the title "bishop" was then reserved.

Many Anglican divines of the sixteenth and early seventeenth centuries (as Richard Field) affirmed that bishops did not excel presbyters in "a distinct power of order," but that their dignity rested merely upon the need of order, unity, and peace in the church. They upheld the mandatory power of the bishops over the presbyters as fitting and profitable, for they believed inequality to be of the nature of all government. Nevertheless, there is nothing arbitrary about their conception of ecclesiastical polity. Hooker clearly pointed out that circumstances of episcopal pride and tyranny might give the Church "urgent cause" to abolish the power of bishops and sometimes—as in the case of Beza—"very great and sufficient reason" could be found "to allow ordination made without a bishop." The episcopate, in short, might be of the *bene esse,* but was not of the *esse,* of the Church.

The general position of the early Anglicans is well represented by George Downham, the Bishop of Derry. In his *Defense* of 1611 he claimed that since episcopacy had the sanction of the apostles, it was a "divine ordinance." But this, he contended, did not entail the conclusion that it "should be generally, perpetually, immutably, necessarily observed, so as no other form of government may in no case be admitted."

During the Elizabethan era the Anglican theologians held that the episcopal polity, which limited the power of ordination to the bishop, had apostolic warrant, and the unique positions of Timothy and Titus in the primitive Christian communities were cited as examples. Following this tradition, the civil and ecclesiastical laws of England forbade any to hold benefices who had not first received episcopal ordination. A few exceptions were certainly made, but they served rather to exemplify the leniency of practice than the abrogation of the law. Indeed, the early Anglicans, for the most part, regarded presbyterian orders as valid but irregular. They held that this irregularity, in breaking from the tradition of the Church, could be defended by the urgency and necessity of the Reformation, where there were no bishops who espoused the reformed cause. Moreover, the change in polity was possible because, as Hooker clearly pointed out, the "whole visible Church," and not the episcopate, "is the true, original subject of all power." Theologians, like Lancelot Andrewes, distinguished between "the true nature and essence of the Church," which was accorded to the Reformed churches, and "the integrity or perfection of a church," which was denied them.[3]

---

[3]From the point of view of the modern discussion of the problem, it is essential to keep a number of things in mind.

(1). The origins of the Christian ministry are so wrapped in obscurity, that no form of polity can exclusively claim the sanction of the apostles or the primitive Church.

(2). Paul regarded the exercise of preaching, teaching, and ruling in the community as *charismata,* or divine gifts, rather than as formal offices.

In the seventeenth century the defence of episcopacy was shifted from this argument of tradition and apostolic sanction to one of immutable, divine right. It is not altogether surprising that the Anglican writers should have answered absolutes with absolutes. Perhaps nothing was more characteristic of the century than the assertion of exaggerated claims and of artificial laws. This is evident in the literature and art of the period, but it is particularly true of the theory and practice of government. The Stuarts found that to rule without a Parliament was frequently less embarrassing, and always more immediately practical, than to rule with one. In a similar way, an extreme form of prelacy for the Church seemed a fitting concomitant of the Stuart policy in temporal government. Bishops might find the assertion of divine right as useful as kings had found it. In the realm of ecclesiastical polity a theory was elaborated to suit the occasion. It was imagined that the imposition of an arbitrary uniformity on the Church might prove an impregnable rock against the growing Puritan power. Indeed, as the struggle of Royalist and Puritan grew more critical, intolerance and absolutism became more completely the guiding principles of both parties. The wise sense of historical convenience, which had characterised the Elizabethan era, was now overthrown for absolutes in theory and practice. In this no ecclesiastic was more completely the child of his age than William

(3). Since prophets were regarded in high esteem by the Early Church, prophetic utterances often preceded appointment to offices and special duties.

(4). While there was no uniform polity in the primitive Church, it is probable that the general Jewish pattern of a ruling sanhedrin of elders was followed. These elders (or bishops as they were called) were appointed and ordained by the apostles, who exercised some authority over them. The successors of these elders were generally chosen by the community, and ordained by the remaining elders.

(5). The rise of the mon-episcopate was a late, second-century development. The unique place of authority over the elders of local churches, which is accorded to Timothy and Titus in the Pastoral Epistles and assumed by The Elder in the Johannine Letters, may have something to do with its development. But the practical necessity of having a single head of the ruling college of elders is probably more responsible for the growth of episcopal power.

Laud, from whose pen came many clear and determined statements of Apostolical Succession, defending the episcopate *jure
divino*.

The assertion of this doctrine by the Anglican divines was
important not only for the defence of the Church against the
Puritans, but also against the Roman Catholics. Archbishop Laud
was at pains to show that episcopal authority derives immediately
from God, and not by mediation through the Pope. Here we
have an analogy with the divine right of kings. Just as the temporal rulers denied the Pope's power in the secular sphere and
asserted that their jurisdiction was directly from God and not
indirectly through the Pope, so the ecclesiastics claimed on the
same grounds to be free from papal control. This clearly distinguished the Anglican from the Roman doctrine of Apostolical
Succession. With Cyprian, Laud and his followers asserted that
what constituted a true Church was the unbroken succession of
its bishops from the apostles, and not its dependence upon the
Roman See.

One other element in the teaching of Laud may be mentioned,
to show that he did not regard Apostolical Succession as the sole
test of a true Church. He says, "Beside the order of Bishops running down (in succession) from the beginning, there is required
consanguinitas doctrinae, that the doctrine be allied in blood to
that of Christ and his apostles." He cites the ancient Greek
Father, Irenæus, to the same effect, and shows it is possible for
a church in the direct succession to err. With Vincent of Lerins,
he regarded "antiquity, universality, and consent," as the final
test of truth.

Two centuries later the doctrine of Apostolical Succession was
revived, but under circumstances altogether different. It was championed by the Tractarians, not in opposition to the Puritans, but

to the State. The Oxford High Churchmen found the doctrine both strategic and timely. They rested the Church's right to be independent of the State upon the assumption that authority over the Church derived directly from Christ and the apostles, through the succession of the bishops. The appeal of history came at an opportune moment. The Romantic Revival had fostered in men's minds a love of the past, and reaction against the excesses of the French Revolution had led to a reverence and respect for time-honored institutions. Apostolical Succession gave the Tractarians a powerful historical defence for their claim, that the authority of the Church is completely independent of the State.

The use made of the doctrine in these two historical periods well exemplifies the truth and falsity of the contention. Insofar as Christianity is an historical religion, which affirms the ultimate meaning of history, the unbroken continuity of the Church's authority and tradition is basic to its doctrine. The life in Christ is not something that can be thought out by man: it rests upon revelation, not upon nature. Christianity is the dynamic Word of God, which is handed down by the Church to successive generations. Men meet Christ not in their fanciful imaginings, but in their fellow Christians. From this arises the overwhelming importance of the historical continuity of the Christian tradition of life and thought. The Church's claim to be independent of every other realm of life must necessarily rest upon this unbroken succession. Insofar as the Tractarians saw and affirmed this, they were true to their Christian profession.

On the other hand, the claim that an order of bishops, distinct from presbyters, existed from New Testament times and hence has a divine sanction is more than dubious. It may have been a convenient answer to an equally arbitrary contention of the Puritans. While that explains, it cannot excuse, its error.

Apostolical Succession, however, was not regarded by the Tractarians as the only mark of a true Church. The position of Laud
was revived. John Newman, who later became a convert to the
Roman Church, claimed, during his Anglican days, that the
Church must conform to apostolic doctrine. By this he meant
the creeds and decisions of the universal councils of the Church
during the early period. Furthermore, he was unwilling to limit
the voice of the Church to the dead past. He contended that the
Church embodied a prophetic tradition and developed its faith
through the centuries, though exactly how to determine the
validity of this tradition was an open question.[4]

Other aspects of the nature of the Church engaged the attention of the Tractarians. They strenuously tried to avoid divorcing
the Church visible from the Church invisible, as if they were
two distinct realities. Rather did they contend that these were
really two aspects of one and the same thing. The outward form,
said Newman, is the guide to that which is truly spiritual, "since
faith and love and joy and peace cannot be seen." In this way
they tried to recapture the organic unity of the Church's outward
form with its inner reality.

This sense of the Church, having a divine foundation, filled
with the divine life, and preserving an unbroken historical succession through the ages, is characteristic of modern Anglicanism.
In the Church of England, however, there are many parties, some
upholding an extreme view of the doctrine of Apostolical Suc-

[4]The dogmatic decisions of the Anglican Church, after the Reformation, were
embodied in the Thirty-nine Articles, which had a definitely Calvinistic note, and
claimed that the Holy Scripture was the final authority in matters of dogma. It
was against this rather Protestant tendency that Newman wrote his famous Tract
90, which aroused a storm of opposition in the Church. His main thesis, upheld
by reasoning that was more brilliant than accurate, was that these Articles were
directed more against the abuses of Rome, than against the Catholic conception
of the Church, which rested the final authority with the General Councils and
with tradition.

cession, and some adopting a more liberal position. It is true that the present form of the establishment may seem an historical anomaly, since atheists and dissenters in Parliament have a part in its temporal government. No satisfactory solution of the relations of Church and State has yet been reached. Nevertheless, the leaders of Anglicanism are vividly aware of the Church as something more than a state department of religion. Constantly through modern Anglican literature, the phrase, "the continuity of the incarnation," can be found to describe the Church. By this is meant that the Church embodies the divine life, incarnate in Jesus Christ, mediated through the sacraments, and manifest to some degree in the life of the Christian community. It rests upon a divine foundation and has its treasure in the spiritual heritage of the ages.[5]

EASTERN ORTHODOXY

A close connection exists today between the Anglican and Eastern Orthodox Churches. Limits of space have prevented our dealing with the long development of the Eastern churches,[6] and we can describe only their most characteristic modern trend, which has an affinity with Anglicanism. The theologian, Bul-

[5]See further the section on the Church in the Report of the Commission on Christian Doctrine in the Church of England, pp. 98 ff. (1938).

[6]The final separation of the Eastern and Latin churches can conveniently be dated in 1054, when they published anathemas against each other. This event brought to a climax a rift which had been developing for several centuries. To the cultural and geographic differences between the two churches was added the struggle for supremacy between the Pope and the Patriarch of Constantinople. Finally, in reply to a letter from the Patriarch, who was seeking some settlement of the outstanding issues (*e.g.,* the use of unleavened bread in the Mass, and the addition of the *filioque* to the Creed), the Pope, Leo IX, wrote a caustic rejoinder. He threatened that he would not "seethe the kid in its mother's milk," but would "scrub its mangey hide with biting vinegar and salt." When the Patriarch refused to comply with the Roman demands, the papal legates laid an anathema upon the high altar of Saint Sophia, in Constantinople, and the Eastern Church replied with a counter-excommunication. This rift in the relations between the two churches has continued to the present day.

gakov, aptly describes this tenor of Orthodox thought when he writes, "The Church of Christ is not an institution; it is a new life with Christ and in Christ, guided by the Holy Spirit." The final authority in dogma is not regarded as the Holy Scriptures, but as the general, universal consciousness of the whole Church—an idea summed up in the Russian word *sobornost*. It must be noted, however, that along with this view which appeals to the traditions of the Fathers and the consciousness of the whole Church, there is another position which claims that the episcopal hierarchy, as well as having pastoral and spiritual jurisdiction, has also the ultimate authority in matters of dogma.

In their former development the Eastern churches have largely been national. They have had a close alliance with such states as Byzantium, Russia, and Rumania. The long period of Turkish domination in the Balkan Peninsula, and the autocratic policy of the Russian Tzars, deprived the Church of its independence, and frequently led to a somewhat servile acceptance of secular government. Modern persecution, particularly in Russia, has awakened the Church to a new consciousness of itself, which finds expression in the stress upon its divine character, its apostolic foundation, and its sacramental life. "The Church," to quote His Beatitude, Chrysostom, the Archbishop of Athens, "is a divinely constituted Society or foundation." It is at once visible and invisible; its members united in one body by an invisible bond of grace, and yet outwardly sharing a common belief and participating in the sacraments. As a visible community it is infallible, possessing the gift of the Holy Spirit; and it is one, united in its internal life with Christ as its Head. Its true unity is not a unity of organisation upon earth, but "a unity transcending space and time." From this are excluded heretics and schismatics, who have no part in it. Finally, the Church is apostolic. "Through the divinely constituted Hierarchy, and so alone, this Church is connected by unbroken succession with the Apostles and keeps the deposit committed unto it by them."

The emphasis upon the infallible authority of the Church and the truth of the Holy Tradition defined by the Church's councils clearly differentiates Eastern Orthodoxy from Protestantism, and makes one of the most formidable obstacles in the efforts to unite non-Roman Christendom. It is closely associated with the assumption that the mystical and empirical Churches cannot be differentiated, but in some sense are identical. The visible Orthodox Church claims to be the actual Body of Christ on earth, or as Androutsos, the Orthodox theologian has said, "The Orthodox Church is the only true and natural continuation of the undivided Church, bearing the promise and validity of her invisible Head."

Eastern Orthodoxy has always had a vivid sense of the Church as a transcendent reality, in which, so to say, time stands still. The unutterable beauty of the ritual and the music of the Eastern liturgy, which reaches its climax in the Easter services, most nearly approaches pure spirit. It lifts the believer into another world, in which the unity of the faithful of all times and places is dramatically apprehended. This constant miracle of the Church's life is made possible by the unbroken succession of the hierarchy and sacraments which reach back to the Incarnation. In its inner meaning, however, it transcends the historical, and pentrates mysteriously into the world beyond.

AMERICAN PROTESTANTISM

There is no single idea of the Church common to American Protestants. Among the vast number of independent ecclesiastical bodies some maintain doctrines derived directly from Europe; others, while tracing their descent from parent bodies in foreign lands, have modified their ideas under the pressure of American thought and life; others, again, have developed their own positions within the stream of American culture. From the point of view of the historian, therefore, it is impossible to talk about the idea of the Church in American Protestantism, because diversity of opinion and varied local character are most typical of the religious scene. Nevertheless, there are some general trends which characterised the development of American Protestantism and distinguish it from the religious situation in other countries.

The three forces that have moulded the development of the idea of the Church in America have been the traditions of Calvinism, of the Reformation sects, and of the Enlightenment. From the first of these comes the concept of the Holy Community, in which the visible Church and the State are conterminous. This was the pattern characteristic of colonial Massachusetts, where the Church was established. The founders of that colony were adherents of the Church of England with Puritan sympathies. They did not wish to separate from the national Church, rather did they want to reform its corruptions. They inherited the idea of a religious community which would have the two-fold aspect of Church and State. In the new environment, however, they modified their Calvinistic ideal by making the Congregational polity, rather than the Presbyterian, the established one. This was partly due to their contact with the Plymouth Colony, which was founded by Congregationalists who had emigrated from the English congregation under John Robinson in Leyden.

The second factor in the early American situation was the reaction against this establishment by the Baptists, the Quakers, and other sects. One of the foremost champions of the idea of religious toleration and the separation of Church and State was Roger Williams, who was characterised by his opponent, Cotton

Mather, as "a preacher that had less light than fire." Outraged by what he called "the Bloudy Tenent of Persecution" in the Bay colony, Roger Williams founded the Providence plantation (1635), which later developed into the Rhode Island colony. Basic to his idea was the principle that "God requireth not an uniformity of Religion to be enacted and enforced in any civil state." He claimed, "True civility and Christianity may both flourish in a state or kingdom, notwithstanding the permission of divers and contrary consciences, either Jew or Gentile."

The third element in the American scene has been the Enlightenment. Under the influence of Jefferson the complete separation of Church from State was finally achieved in the national government, through the passing of the first Amendment to the Constitution. After the Revolution the principle of establishment in the various states died a lingering death, becoming finally extinct when it was abandoned by Massachusetts in 1834. With the triumph of the thinking of the Enlightenment government was no longer regarded as having a religious basis or needing religious direction: rather was it founded upon reason and the natural law. Religion was looked upon as a matter of private inclination rather than of civic concern. It is true that the government accepted a certain religious responsibility by exempting the property of all religious institutions from taxation. Nevertheless, the predominant idea of the Church was of a voluntary association that had the right to determine its own faith and laws.

American Protestantism developed through the interaction of these three forces, and the situation was further complicated by the general trend of American culture. A conscious break with the European past and a suspicion of tradition marked the temper of the American mind after the Revolution, while the conditions of the frontier made for a stern practicability and a mode of work and thought experimental and empirical. Furthermore, the successive streams of immigration from Europe brought an increasing variety of religious cultures and traditions, which even yet have not been fully assimilated.

Out of this mêlée came the emphasis upon the churches rather than upon the Church. In a country that lacked a unity of cultural tradition and any single religious basis for the Federal Constitution, it was only natural that religious life should be marked by a variety of autonomous churches and denominations. This diversity in organisation was further characterised by the spread of the Congregational polity, which to some extent affected even those communions in which a centralised form of government was traditional. The support of the Church rested almost entirely with the local congregation. The small community possessed the property, called and financed the pastor, and administered the church affairs. Thus the consciousness of being an isolated Christian fellowship rather than a part of the Church Universal easily developed.

The stress upon the particular congregation has a philosophic root in the American tendency to see things in the concrete and to regard empirical phenomena as the most real. The sense of the Church as the one transcendent body of Christ has largely given way to the idea of churches. The Church is regarded as an abstraction, derived from a consideration of a number of particular congregations—an idea clearly worked out by the early Congregationalist writer, John Robinson. In this stress on churches, American thought has lost something of great and permanent value in Christianity. It is not a matter of having either The Church or the churches: it is rather a question of maintaining both, for they are complementary and not exclusive realities. The ultimate meaning of the churches is The Church, in which they participate and are grounded. The churches are not merely local expressions of cultural life or even aggregations of believers. They are historical manifestations of the people of God. Yet The Church, the transcendent unity of The Faith, has only historical meaning and existence, when it is embodied in the churches and denominations which share its life and witness to its divine origin and gospel.

Perhaps the most notable feature in this development of the churches was the democratic emphasis. Central authority tended to be weak and congregations were for the most part independent. When any serious conflict arose secession was the general practice. One has only to glance down the most recent census of the religious bodies in the U. S. A. to note the great number of autonomous denominations which from time to time have split from the parent communions. Under this democratic influence the laity have assumed a significant rôle in the government and organisation of the churches. Even those bodies with a more autocratic tradition have become imbued with the spirit of American political theory. In the Protestant Episcopal Church, for instance, the laity have been given a large representation in the Lower House of General Convention, and the minister is called by the vestry (a lay body elected by the congregation) and not appointed by the bishop. Here, again, the support of the church by the congregation has been important. There has been no such European custom as patronage, and the financial independence of the congregation has led to the demand of the laity to have an adequate part in church government.

A further trend away from the idea of the Church as an institution has appeared in the religious revivals which have periodically swept through America. Beginning with the Great Awakening in the middle of the eighteenth century, and con-

tinuing in succession to the present day, they have given American
religion one of its most typical features. Periods of apathy and
irreligion have been superseded by extremes of religious enthusiasm and hysteria. These revivals cut across denominational
boundaries and made vivid appeals to all nominal Christians.
They fostered a religion of direct experience, presupposing neither
the necessity of the Church nor of any adequate theology. Though
their success has never been significant within the churches of
the older tradition, as the Episcopalian and Presbyterian, they
have caused temporary secessions (*e.g.,* the Cumberland Presbyterians), and have revitalised religion among the other denominations. Particularly on the frontier have the revivals played an
important rôle; they offered a realistic and direct religious experience to those who cared nothing for tradition and to whom
the Church and its sacraments were often meaningless.

Though the divisive temper of American Protestantism had
been most marked since the Union, the idea of the Holy Community has not died out. Through the influence of the Enlightenment, however, and the general force of American life, it has
reappeared in a secularised form and has given American thinking on the Church another of its distinctive features. The Church
is looked upon as an agency for promoting the moral life of the
community and for advancing the social interests of the underprivileged. This conception underlies many of the sociological
studies of the Church, which have appeared in recent years. In
attempting to analyse and estimate the place of the Church in
the community, the spiritual factor, which does not lend itself
to scientific inquiry, is often neglected. Religion tends to be regarded as moral virtue, which it is the duty of the Christian
fellowship to exemplify and enforce. Much of American Protestantism is actively concerned with prevailing social conditions.

It looks in hope to the realisation of the Kingdom of God in history and under the form of the Social Gospel preaches the Christian duty of "building the Kingdom."

Much of this emphasis upon spreading the Kingdom of God in the world is due to the influence of the German theologian Ritschl. He attempted to distinguish between the terms "church" and "Kingdom of God," maintaining that the former is the worshipping congregation, while the latter is the body of those who "act mutually from love and so produce the community of moral dispositions and moral goods, which extends in all possible degrees to the limits of the human race." Ritschl laid practically no emphasis upon the future Kingdom that God will reveal, but he stressed the actual existence of the Kingdom on earth wherever love and brotherhood extend. This liberal Christianity, while it avoids the Roman Catholic dogma, which identifies an earthly institution with the Kingdom of God, nevertheless runs the danger of thinking purely in terms of man's moral achievements. It neglects the element of crisis and the anticipation of God's activity in history.

This moral activism finds expression in the great variety of activities, in which the local churches are engaged. They are busy centres of social life. They provide healthy recreation by dances and gym classes; they hold discussion groups, and help to alleviate suffering in the community by various forms of social service. They are alive to many of the vital problems in modern society; and such topics as sex and war and poverty are frankly discussed.

Among the more radical groups, direct participation in politics has been advocated from time to time, and the pressure of the churches in such issues as slavery and social legislation, and in the less fortunate experiment of prohibition, has been very powerful. The basic idea of the Church that lies behind this somewhat secularised idea of the Holy Community is one in which it is regarded as the agent for building the moral Kingdom of God upon earth. The place of the sacraments in religious life is neglected: the Church is not the divine institution that mediates the grace of God, lifting the fellowship of believers into the mystery of the world beyond. Rather is the stress laid upon the will of God as personal and social holiness, which it is the Christian duty to establish in the world.

All these trends in American religious life find their consummation in the community church, perhaps the most representative feature of American Protestantism. It is interdenominational, drawing its members and ministers from many diverse communions. It is a separate, autonomous congregation, self-supporting, and democratic in its government. It shows concern for the needs of the community and preaches a gospel of moral justice and the corporate prosperity of America.

A last trend which has received increasing emphasis since the beginning of the twentieth century has been toward church unity. Between the years of 1906 and 1933 some eleven unions have been consummated among twenty-two denominations, affecting over eight million Christians. It is highly significant, therefore, that the initiative for one phase of the ecumenical movement (Faith and Order) came from America.

Even more important than organic union has been the tendency toward the closer co-operation of the churches in practical affairs. The formation of the Federal Council of the Churches of Christ in America in 1908 bears witness to this. By presenting a united front the Federal Council attempts actively to relate Christianity to every sphere of American society. Its commissions have done great service in making detailed surveys of the state of the churches, and of social, economic, and educational aspects of the national life. The intervention of the Council (along with Jewish and Roman Catholic commissions) in the steel strike of 1923 is one of its most notable triumphs.

Perhaps the most important element in the creation of the Federal Council is the idea of federation. Rather than attempting to unite the churches by means of an organic unity the Federal Council, following American political theory, has succeeded in providing a means whereby the existing denominations can co-operate effectively without abandoning their traditions and their existing polities. This concept of federation is probably one of the most fruitful avenues of approach toward solving the problem of the reunion of Christendom.

There are many elements involved in the American desire for unity. It has, first, a practical basis. The Federal Council aims to represent and declare the common conscience of the churches upon important issues which concern the social order and the moral life. Then again, this ideal for closer co-operation has derived not a little of its force from the common Christian experience, which has been fostered by the American Revivals. These were essentially undenominational in outlook and expression and bore their fruit in the joint movements for Christian endeavour and missionary activity.

One of the salient factors which has made this trend possible has been the corporate life which American Protestants have been forced to lead. Christians in one church cannot live in intimate contact with those of another without discovering that denominational differences are often insignificant. To the American mind many of the issues which formerly divided the churches have lost their meaning. European in origin and expression, these causes of separation seem to belong to an obsolete past.

In a land where many diverse groups have had to live the same social life together there naturally arose the belief that no one in particular has a monopoly on religious truth. While in Europe the social background of the denominations is still apparent, in America these divisions have ceased to exist. Methodists, Presbyterians, Congregationalists, Baptists, and Episcopalians are the same type of people, leading the same type of life. In such circumstances a common Christian heritage is of more significance than denominational rivalries. Added to this is the fact that each town and village cannot have a church of every particular tradition, and the moving population finds itself forced to be as much at home in one Protestant church as another.

A significant parable for American Protestantism is Riverside Church, in New York. Although it has a Baptist tradition, it recruits its members from every sect and church, and is largely supported by those who are opposed to denominational differences. It is a symbol of American Protestantism looking for an adequate expression. The church itself is a Gothic building, in which mediæval symbolism has been combined with modern convenience. It is not, however, the spirit of the Middle Ages that has overcome its members: they are not romantically looking back upon the Catholic unity of the thirteenth century. They are expressing in an architecture, that will always remain foreign to America, the desire to live a corporate Christian life, which is at once distinct from the secular life of New York with its skyscrapers, and yet more full and varied than the simplicity of the New England tradition. Travel in Europe has inspired them with the idea of the cathedral. American Protestantism has outgrown the pioneer spirit of the Colonial Meeting House. Leisure and luxury are demanding their part in the religious life, but the creative spirit of Protestant Christianity is still struggling to find an adequate expression for its genius.

<h2>REUNION</h2>

The twentieth century has witnessed an ever increasing emphasis upon the reunion of the churches. While there is great diversity of opinion upon the kind of union that is necessary or practicable, there is a fairly common consciousness that the closer co-operation of the churches is an immediate duty. This interest in reunion has a variety of roots. In the first place, the pressing practical problems of the mission field have made the divisions of Christendom seem not only wasteful but actually harmful. The gospel of one Lord, one faith, and one Baptism can hardly be effectively preached to those of other faiths by a number of rival denominations whose activities overlap. It is highly significant, therefore, that the first move toward ecumenical thinking was taken at the Edinburgh Missionary Conference in 1910. It was at this gathering that there came the inspiration for the Faith and Order Movement, which was initiated the same year at the General Convention of the Protestant Episcopal Church in the U. S. A.

The anti-Christian forces of the modern world, the totalitarian state, Communism, and the scientific secularism of a "brave new world," have all challenged the foundations of the gospel of Jesus Christ. By a recognition of their common allegiance, which far transcends their differences, Christians have been brought together, and have felt the earnest need for presenting a united front in thought no less than in action, against these movements that threaten the very existence of the churches. Finally, the world-consciousness, which the Great War and the rapid development of communication have forced upon us, together with the ideas of toleration which characterised the Liberal Era, have contributed to the sense of Christian unity.

It is important to realise, however, that the most successful unions between the churches have been brought about where there has been more than a general awareness of a common Christian heritage. The unions concluded among various denominations in Germany (1922), Scotland (1929), Canada (1925), China (1927), and the U. S. A. owed not a little of their success to the fact that the churches participating shared both the same national life and very similar Protestant beliefs and forms of worship. The issue at stake in the Scottish union of 1929 was related neither to faith nor liturgy, but concerned the exercise of patronage, by which ministers were formerly forced on unwilling congregations. In 1733 and 1761 secessions from the established Church of Scotland occurred, and the two schisms opposing patronage united in 1847 in the United Presbyterian Church. Four years earlier the Free Church of Scotland had been founded by a group of evangelical ministers and laymen, whose stern and uncompromising protest against the spirit of liberalism led them to resent the foisting of "moderate" ministers upon congregations which adhered to more traditional forms of piety. In 1900 the Free Church (with the exception of a small minority who came to be known as the "Wee Frees") joined with the United Presbyterian Church and formed the United Free Church of Scotland. Finally, this body was reconciled with the established Church in 1929, and the Patronage Act provided that the congregations of the Church of Scotland should have the right of electing their own ministers.

The union in Germany in 1817, by which the Lutheran and Reformed Churches were joined in the largest of the German territorial churches, The Evangelical Church of the Old Prussian

Union, was similarly little concerned with matters of belief. It was agreed that the Reformed congregations should continue to use the Heidelberg Catechism, while the others should retain Luther's Smaller Catechism. A variety of liturgical use was also permitted. In 1922 a somewhat more loose federation of the German churches was formed in The German Evangelical Church Federation, but there was no legislation concerning matters of faith or worship.

The attempt of the State since the 1933 Revolution to enforce unity upon the twenty-eight territorial churches of Germany has not yet met with success. It has been complicated by the political situation and the strife between the Confessional Church and the State. While no one would dare predict the future of the Evangelical Church in Germany, it is clear that persecution has been a tremendous factor in bringing the Church to a consciousness of its real unity.

With the formation of the United Church of Canada in 1925, Presbyterians, Methodists, and Congregationalists were joined together, though a not insignificant body of Presbyterians remained outside the union. The doctrinal statement, which followed the general lines of the Brief Statement of the Reformed Faith (Presbyterian Church in the U. S. A.), was not made binding on the ministers, and the issue of church polity was resolved by a compromise between the existing systems of the three denominations.

The formation of the Church of Christ in China in 1927 is of peculiar interest. It is the largest organic union that Protestantism has effected including about one-third of the Protestants of China. Congregationalists, Baptists, Methodists, Presbyterians, Reformed, and United Brethren are numbered among the uniting bodies.

On the doctrinal side the basis of reunion was severely simple. It consisted of three articles of belief, confessing faith in Christ as Redeemer, in His Kingdom and Church and belief in the inspiration and authority of the Scriptures, and the Apostles' Creed. While the General Assembly approved of the "Christian Message" of the Jerusalem Conference, it was not made binding on the whole Church. The administration of the Church is conducted along lines that combine elements of the Congregational and Presbyterian polities and the experiment has proved of significant value in solving the problems created by the great number and variety of English and American Protestant missions in China.

The unions presupposed the two important elements of a common Protestant heritage and the same national life. This fundamental basis of agreement was able to overcome the less significant obstacles to union.

Another form of close co-operation can be seen in the connection that sister churches have with one another in various lands. The Lambeth Conference is an illuminating example. Every ten years the bishops of the Anglican and Protestant Episcopal Churches meet together to confer on the vital issues of the day. While the Lambeth pronouncements do not have the form of church law, their moral influence is great and even extends beyond the bounds of the Anglican Communion.

Closely allied with this type of international relationship is the recognition by various churches of the orders and sacraments of others. In 1922 the Church of England and the Church of Sweden reached such an agreement, and a similar position exists between the Anglican, the Eastern Orthodox, and the Old Catholic Communions. While in none of these cases can there be said to be any union of the churches, mutual recognition is a step toward closer co-operation.[7]

Where church union has so far woefully failed is among churches which hold mutually exclusive positions on faith and practice. No union with the Church of Rome is possible without submission to the Pope, because the Roman Church maintains that their particular hierarchy, summed up in the papacy, is alone of divine institution. But the other churches of Christendom stalwartly refuse to acknowledge this. A similar situation is evident in the unwillingness of Presbyterians to accept the uncompromising attitude of Anglicans on episcopacy. In the same way no close relationship can be achieved with the Southern Baptists in the U. S. A. by any denominations which fail to allow that adult baptism by immersion is the divinely appointed manner of initiation into the Christian community. Or again, the Evangelical Lutheran Synod of Missouri is equally convinced that the recognition of its form of doctrine is a *sine qua non* to any proposals for union.

It is this situation which creates the most formidable obstacle in the path of the Ecumenical Movement. Churches which have a fairly similar tradition and national life are not averse from union; and those with the same or similar forms of church government are often willing to recognise sister churches in other lands. But there are insuperable difficulties in trying to discover any common ground among denominations which define the nature of the Church from mutually exclusive premises. A study of the conclusions reached at Lausanne in 1927 will ably demonstrate this.

The delegates of the World Conference on Faith and Order,

[7]Another most important contribution to the problem of the reunion of the churches is to be found in the *Outline for a Reunion Scheme for the Church of England and the Evangelical Free Churches of England,* which the Joint Conference of Anglicans and Free Churchmen have issued (S. C. M. Press, London, 1938).

representing some 108 non-Roman communions, met to consider the whole series of problems concerning the faith, the Church, the sacraments, and the ministry, which bore upon the issue of reunion. In the final report,[8] the section which dealt with the nature of the Church stated the points of agreement and of divergence. There was unanimity on five points: viz., (1) that the Church was constituted by the will of God and not the will of men; (2) that it had as its head Jesus Christ; (3) that it was the means of man's reconciliation with God, and was united "in love and service to be His witnesses and fellow workers in the extension of His will on earth until His Kingdom come in glory"; (4) that it was one, holy, catholic and apostolic; and (5) that it was known by a number of marks, such as its possession and acknowledgment of the Word of God in the Scriptures, its profession of faith in the Incarnation, its administration of the sacraments, its ministry, and its being a fellowship "in prayer, in worship, in all the means of grace, in the pursuit of holiness, and in the service of man."

While this measure of agreement with its emphasis upon the Church as a divine creation was significant, it gave no possible criterion for the testing of opposing claims. It was the lowest common denominator of belief about the Church, and not the norm. What it excluded was of more importance than what it included, for it did not venture to touch the basic issue, "How is the grace of God mediated to man?" That is where every definition of the Church has to start, for in the answer to that

[8]It is important to realise that the delegates to these Faith and Order Conferences (Lausanne, 1927, and Edinburgh, 1937), while duly elected by the participating communions, have no authority to commit the church they represent to any of the final decisions. The reports of the Conference are referred to the different communions, which discuss them in their authoritative councils. Replies are then drafted and forwarded to the Continuation Committee of the World Conference on Faith and Order. A significant selection of the responses of the Churches to the Edinburgh Conference has been published by Macmillan (1934) under the title *Convictions,* edited by Canon L. Hodgson.

question is given the criterion by which fellow companies of professing Christians can be known and acknowledged. If it is believed that the distinctive element in Christianity is a quality of life which is the free gift of the Spirit of God independent of the mediation of any particular institution, then the reunion of the churches would be unnecessary, indeed, it might even be harmful. As a matter of fact, few, if any, Christians maintain this, though all make allowance for God's extraordinary gifts of grace. There is, for instance, the Roman Catholic dogma of the soul and body of the Church, and the Calvinist doctrine of "uncovenanted mercies" for those outside the visible institution. Practically all Christians, however (save the Friends), hold that the ordinary means of grace are the faith and sacraments of a visible church, which can be recognised by some definite marks. The vital issue is to discover these marks, without which no fellowship or institution can truly be called "Church."

The statement of differences in the Lausanne Report was not very lengthy and did not put the problem in the requisite clarity. It stated, among other things, that some held the tradition of the Church to be determinative for faith, while others held Scripture was alone sufficient. There was a divergence of opinion on the meaning of the Visible Church, the expression of which some maintain had been determined by Christ and was unchangeable. Furthermore, some claimed a special form of ministry to be necessary to the Visible Church, and there was difference on the issue whether the Church (as already described in the five points of agreement) was to be found in all or some of the existing communions.

A more basic distinction in the way of looking at the Church was clearly brought out in the report of the Edinburgh Conference of 1937.

"Behind all particular statements of the problem of corporate union lie deeply divergent conceptions of the Church. For the want of any more accurate terms this divergence might be described as the contrast between "authoritarian" and "personal" types of Church.

"We have, on the one hand, an insistence upon a divine given-ness, in the Scriptures, in orders, in creeds, in worship.

"We have, on the other hand, an equally strong insistence upon the individual experience of Divine grace, as the ruling principle of the "gathered" Church, in which freedom is both enjoyed as a religious right and enjoined as a religious duty."

Behind this distinction lies the age-old struggle between the institutional and the spiritual Church. Perhaps the history of the past has demonstrated that neither emphasis is complete in itself. They are complementary rather than antithetical truths.

The fundamental question to which all these differences go back is, "What is necessary for a Church? What is of such vital moment that we cannot give it up?" Here many of the Christian bodies are not themselves agreed and often divergencies of opinion cut across denominational lines. But some examples may be illuminating. In general, the Anglicans and the Eastern Orthodox insist that a necessary mark of the Church is the episcopate, which, it is claimed, stands in a direct line of descent from the Apostles. The Roman Church holds to the papacy, others to baptism by immersion, others to specific doctrinal standards. Then, again, there is the emphasis of the Barthian theology which has recaptured Luther's stress upon faith and the preaching of the Word of God, as the essential marks of the Church. Finally, there are those who demand that freedom is basic to the experience of the divine Grace.

How are we to test which of these marks is valid? Is it sufficient to hold blindly to our particular tradition and to deny others? These are the essential questions to answer before any steps can be taken toward organic union—union, that is, which embraces a variety of former denominations in a single, visible Church with one ministry and one formulation of faith.

In attempting to solve these˙problems one vital factor must be borne in mind. The marks of the Church which are most seriously contested are those very points where our faith in the Church as a more than human institution is centred. For this reason the real meaning of these marks is not their purely historical, but their divine, transcendent significance. It is not enough for scholars to prove or disprove that the episcopate was a late development, or that baptism by immersion was a primitive Christian rite, or that any particular formula of faith embodies an interpretation of Scripture which is not historically correct. These outward signs stand for something which transcends history; they have a sacramental significance, and they can neither be identified with nor divorced from the spiritual reality they are seen to signify. Perhaps the most fruitful approach is to recognise that in the varieties of our historical tradition the grace of God has been mediated to man through many diverse forms and in many different fellowships.

It is from this point of view of mutual recognition that the most significant advances in the Ecumenical Movement have been made. On the more practical side, the recent conference on Life and Work at Oxford has clearly shown that, while there is far from unanimity, there is an important consensus of opinion on the Christian attitude to the basic problems that confront the modern world. Though the reports of the five Oxford commissions do not have the nature of authoritative pronouncements of the different churches, they have given significant direction to Christian thinking on these issues. They evidence a fundamental recognition that the Church has a unique mission to fulfil in the world and rightly demands freedom from all political and social powers to proclaim the Gospel. Furthermore, these reports give vital expression to the need of the various communions to co-operate in definite practical tasks that concern Christian life in the world today.

The Edinburgh conference on Faith and Order showed progress upon Lausanne in at least two directions. In the first place, the basic issues of the federation of the churches and intercommunion were openly discussed in a way that had been impossible at Lausanne. Secondly, the plans for the creation of the World Council of the Churches evidenced the extent to which the various communions were willing to give concrete expression to their mutual recognition of one another. Though fundamental differences in belief about the nature of the Church preclude any organic union on a large scale in the near future, the principle of federation, which underlies this World Council, has been clearly put forward, and, if accepted by the different denominations, will mark very significant progress toward the unity of non-Roman Christendom. Furthermore, it will bring together the two phases of the Ecumenical Movement, "Life and Work" and "Faith and Order," and give them more official recognition in the churches. Though the authority of such a Council will be severely limited, it will present a single voice to speak and act on the major issues that confront the Church in the modern world.

Chapter VIII

CONCLUSION

The course of Christian history we have rapidly surveyed has evidenced a great variety of ideas of the Church, which have been incorporated in many diverse institutions. In the early days of Christianity "Church" meant the fellowship of the new age, the community of those who, even in the present, were the inheritors of the promises made to the prophets, and who looked in hope to the near fulfilment of God's Kingdom. Stress was laid upon the unity of this people, rather than upon the diversity of the local congregations. In the midst of an anti-Christian culture, these believers were bound together by a common allegiance to Christ, which was constantly renewed in the rite of the Eucharist. Their religious vision quickened and deepened their moral perception, and in their life no less than in their faith they stood in contrast to their age and culture.

The recognition of Christianity by the Roman Emperors and the decay of the Western Empire paved the way for significant changes in this primitive conception. The Church became a powerful and universal institution, that had a close relationship with the world. The unity of medieval Europe was the Catholic Church, with its claim to be the Kingdom of God on earth. The guardian of an infallible tradition and revelation, the Church was beyond criticism, and at the apex of its structure stood the papacy. In the drama of the Mass, the central feature of medieval religious life, the Church re-enacted the drama of salvation and brought the life of God to men.

The danger of such claims lay in the inevitable tendency of the Church to become God-defying and to give the sanction of religion to a particular institution and culture. The Church with its contention to be absolute and beyond criticism could not escape the corruption of power and tended to identify its own interests and existence with those of true religion and virtue.

To the early Reformers the Church meant the transcendent community of those who had faith. With prophetic vision they denied the absolute institution which set itself up as God upon earth. The moral vigour of the Reformation expressed itself in its condemnation of the corrupt ecclesiasticism of the late Middle Ages, and the level of Christian life was raised by the stern and austere ethics of the Puritans. But the Reformation Church could not avoid falling a prey to the two social forces which had largely made its triumph possible, the rising nationalism and capitalism. Protestant institutions had not the wealth and power of the old Latin Church and could not effectively assert their independence of economic and political forces. A further danger lay in the attempt to make particular confessional standards or an infallible Bible the absolute and authoritative guide of truth.

Contemporary with the Protestant idea of the Church was the conception of the sect, which came to play a very significant rôle in the development of Christianity in America. The sects were composed largely of dispossessed groups, and stood out in marked opposition to the compromises with the world which the early reformers had been forced to make. Stressing both the purity of morals and of piety, the sects were uncompromising in their attitude toward the State churches, contending that the Church should be separate from the world. The difficulties which faced such a position were those of retreat from the problems of life and of making a particular type of personal ethics absolute. They failed to realise the complexity of man's life in the world and the inevitable relativism of all his decisions. A further dilemma that confronted the sect type of religion was to maintain the high moral and religious standards of the early movement. The tendency was always for later generations to conform to the "Church" type.

With the Enlightenment and the growth of rationalism the idea of the denomination came to the fore. The various Protestant communions came to regard each other with toleration, and stress was laid upon the different churches rather than upon the transcendent unity of The Church. In America particularly, the central place of worship in the Church's life was superseded by activism and the social gospel. The tendency was to think of the Church as one among many institutions for advancing personal happiness and social justice.

The world consciousness awakened by the Great War and by the rapid growth of missionary activity led to the founding of the Ecumenical Movement and a revived interest in the essential unity and religious task of the Church. Within the last decade the churches have resisted the divisive trend of modern culture, which has been precipitated by the rise of the Fascist states. A consciousness of the unique place of the Church and the real unity of its spiritual existence has been clearly evidenced at the Oxford and Edinburgh Conferences of 1937, which ably reflect modern trends of thinking in non-Roman Christianity. Despite the divergence of opinion upon the nature of the Church, there is a common awareness that it is a divine creation, which stands in opposition to the world, and is the guardian of a supreme revelation, that can meet the hour of crisis. Although the Ecumenical Movement lacks the authority of the councils of the early Church and the participating communions retain their autonomy, the plans for the creation of the World Council of the Churches presages to give a not insignificant unity to non-Roman Christendom.

Perhaps the ideal concept of the Church would incorporate the values of each of these types as they have arisen in Christian history. From the early period we gain the vision of the Church as the fellowship of salvation, called by God to live in the New Age, which is the Kingdom and rule of Christ. The Catholic development discloses the idea of the Church as the divine institution powerful to fulfil its mission, and with a close relationship with the world. It guards the Christian tradition and revelation, and renews the unity of its life in the sacrament of the Eucharist. Yet the prophetic genius of Protestantism must too be maintained. The danger must be avoided of making such an institution absolute, or giving religious sanction to any particular culture. From the concept of the sect we see the importance of preserving moral vigour and spiritual freedom in the Church, neglecting neither the religious vision of the poor and dispossessed nor the keen sense of fellowship in a small community. But it must be realised that retreat from the world is an escape from man's problems and not a solution of them, while the difficulty of oversimplifying the Christian life by a system of absolute personal or social ethics must be faced. From the idea of the denomination we appreciate the significance of toleration and the possible solution of the unity of the Church through the federation of existing communions which retain the values of their past traditions. It is well, however, to remember that toleration can so easily lead to indifference. To be truly tolerant does not mean that our *differences* make no *difference*. Finally, from the Ecumenical Movement we gain the much needed emphasis upon the unity of the Church's life, throughout the world and through the ages, and we understand the meaning of the Church as the divine creation, the body of those whom God has called through His Son and sent into the world to do His will. Because the truth of the Christian tradition is vital and not dead, it is embodied in a living community, which preserves, reinterprets, and hands it down to successive generations. In the Church Christianity is made alive.

FOR FURTHER READING

USEFUL SOURCE BOOKS

Ayer, J. C., *A Source Book for Ancient Church History*. 1913.
Coulton, G. G., *Life in the Middle Ages*. 4 vols. 1930.
Dogmatic Canons and Decrees (*of the Roman Catholic Church*). 1912.
McGlothlin, W. J., *Baptist Confessions of Faith*. 1911.
More, P. E., and Cross, F. L., *Anglicanism*. 1935.
Schaff, P., *The Creeds of Christendom*. 3 vols. 1877; revised, 1931.
Thatcher, O. J., and McNeal, E. H., *A Source Book for Medieval History*. 1905.
Walker, W., *The Creeds and Platforms of Congregationalism*. 1893.

PRIMARY WORKS

Augustine, *City of God*.
Bate, H. N., Editor, *Faith and Order*. 1927.
Calvin, *Institutes of the Christian Religion*. Translated by Beveridge. 3 vols. 1845.
Doctrine in the Church of England, Report of the Archbishops' Commission. 1938.
Hodgson, L., Editor, *Convictions*. 1934.
Hooker, R., *Of the Laws of Ecclesiastical Polity*. 3 vols. 1888.
Luther, *Primary Works*. Edited by Wace and Buchheim. 1896.
Report of the Second World Conference on Faith and Order. 1937.
Roberts and Donaldson, Editors, *The Ante-Nicene Fathers*. 1899.
Wesley, J., *Selections from the Writings of John Wesley*. Edited by Welch. 1929.

SECONDARY WORKS

Bevan, E., *Christianity*. 1932.
Brilioth, Y., *The Anglican Revival*. 1933.
Brown, W. A., *Church and State in America*. 1936.
———, *The Church, Catholic and Protestant*. 1935.
Bryce, J., *The Holy Roman Empire*. 1930.

Bulgakov, S., *The Orthodox Church*. 1935.

Cavert, S. M., and Van Dusen, H. P., Editors. *The Church Through Half a Century*. 1936.

Coulton, G. G., *Five Centuries of Religion*. 3 vols. 1923 ff.

Dawson, C., *Medieval Religion*. 1934.

Douglas, H. P., *A Decade of Objective Progress in Church Unity, 1927–1936*. 1937.

Ehrenstrom, N., *Christian Faith and the Modern State*. 1937.

Foakes-Jackson, F. J., *The History of the Christian Church to A.D. 461*. 1924.

Hallam, H., *View of the State of Europe During the Middle Ages*. 2 vols. 1898.

Keller, A., *Church and State on the European Continent*. 1936.

Lindsay, T. M., *The Church and Ministry in the Early Centuries*. 1924.

——, *History of the Reformation*. 2 vols. 1911.

Mackinnon, J., *Calvin and the Reformation*. 1936.

——, *Luther and the Reformation*. 4 vols. 1925.

McGiffert, A. C., *A History of Christian Thought*. 2 vols. 1932.

Micklem, N., Editor, *Christian Worship*. 1936.

Niebuhr, H. R., *The Kingdom of God in America*. 1937.

Patterson, M. W., *A History of the Church of England*. 1912.

Slosser, G. J., *Christian Unity*. 1929.

Streeter, B. H., *The Primitive Church*. 1929.

Sweet, W. W., *The Story of Religions in America*. 1930.

Taylor, H. O., *The Medieval Mind*. 2 vols. 1930.

Thompson, J. W., *History of the Middle Ages*. 1931.

Townsend, W. J., Workman, H. B., and Eays, G., Editors. *A New History of Methodism*. 2 vols. 1909.

Troeltsch, E., *The Social Teaching of the Christian Churches*. 2 vols. 1931.

Underhill, E., *Worship*. 1937.

Visser 'T Hooft, W. A., and Oldham, J., *The Church and Its Function in Society*. 1937.

Walker, W., *A History of the Christian Church*. 1918.

Wand, J. W. C., *A History of the Modern Church*. 1929.

Williams, M., *The Catholic Church in Action*. 1934.

INDEX